One Is More than Un

One Is More than Un

A Personal Growth Book for the Single Adult

by
Debbie Salter

Beacon Hill Press of Kansas City
Kansas City, Missouri

All scripture quotations are from *The Living Bible,* © 1971 by
Tyndale House Publishers, Wheaton, Ill. Used by permission.

Dedication

To

Ruth and Bill, who
convinced me I could;

K.C., N.E. Ind., N. Cent. Ohio, Phila.
district single retreaters who
told me I should;

Mother and Dad who
always knew I would.

Contents

Chapter One

Am I Only One?

I was making my first cross-country trip by car, by myself. My driver's license was still new. So was my behind-the-wheel prowess.

Mr. Craddock, my employer and friend, gave grandfatherly counsel. His silky-white age-crown shook with the nod of his head as he stamped "IMPORTANT" on his conversation with me.

"Be sure you check the oil, the water, the air in your tires before leaving," he cautioned. "And don't forget to have them check the air in your spare tire."

So with his memorized checklist in mind, I drove to my friendly Mobil station with an I've-done-this-so-many-times-before nonchalance and asked, "Would you check the oil, water, gas, tires, and check the air in my spare, too, please." I took furtive looks in my rear view mirror and hoped he didn't ask me where anything was or how much something was supposed to be. Evidently, he didn't need my assistance except to give him my trunk key. Seconds later, he returned to my window, scratching his head.

"Lady, you don't have a spare tire."

I answered him the way any normal, quick-witted woman would.

"Oh?"

When I returned to the office and told Mr. Craddock my story, he scratched his head just like the attendant.

"Debbie, are you sure you don't have a spare tire?"

"He checked. I looked. There's nothing there. Empty."

"Well, we've got to get you a spare tire. I can't have you driving to Kansas City all by yourself without a spare tire."

Instantly he was on the phone, telephoning every service station around, trying to locate or borrow a spare tire. He finally found one . . . at my friendly Mobil station.

I swallowed my pride and drove in. I was relieved to find a different attendant on duty.

"So you're the one without the spare tire," he snickered. I cringed with embarrassment because the story of my female ignorance had spread.

"You sure you don't have a spare tire?" he queried.

"No, I guess not."

"That's very unusual, Miss."

"That's what I understand," I said through my teeth, already tired of this third degree.

"Did you check the well?"

The well. Since I didn't know what it was, I guess I hadn't checked it.

The attendant strutted back to the trunk with an I-knew-it-all-along attitude, lifted the bottom cover to reveal a *well* where a brand new spare tire snugly rested.

I almost made the trip on the shaky possibility that I wouldn't need a spare tire. I almost spent unnecessary money when exactly what I needed was with me all the time. My ignorance did not negate its existence. It just made it unavailable.

This book is dedicated to the proposition that, as singles, some of us are driving around with necessary spare tires in hidden wells.

*   *   *

Sometimes I live in a Noah's Ark world where I feel left over. Tickets sell two for the price of one, but one is *more than* one-half of two. Tables set for quartets make five an inconvenience.

I am a limp to my society. No one expects me to be single. Especially not the salesman who builds his client list from the telephone book. He calls at 5:30 expecting to interrupt a housewife's evening meal preparation. He doesn't realize that the only marriage responsibility I feel toward my apartment is that unless I take the garbage out tonight, I am going to have to fumigate.

"Mrs. Salter?" he asks with his reading-from-step-number-one voice.

I decide not to frustrate him with the information that my mother lives in Kansas City and would he like her number? Besides, there is no step "1-a" for the single client.

"Is Mr. Salter at home?"

Not wanting to take anything for granted, I look around to make sure.

"Not at the moment," I finally decide to say.

"Can you tell me when he will return?"

Tell *him* when he will return? I just want someone to tell me if he's ever going to *arrive!*

Other people try to tell me he should have by now. You know the question. It might come in a circle of Christmas card relatives or when you are introduced to the "I've-heard-so-much-about-you" friends of your parents.

"What's a nice girl like you doing single?"

"How come a nice young man like you isn't married?"

9

Sometimes I want to answer loudly, almost bitterly, "I don't know, but when I find out, I'll tell you." I understand it is meant as a compliment but, like my backhand tennis swing, it usually misses.

Although being one person may be an advantage at a two-for-one sale or when there is room for "one more" on a flight to Los Angeles, society is not usually beneficent toward the single adult. They say we are *only* one without family responsibilities, therefore immature. They say we are *only* one with twice as much freedom; therefore irresponsible. They say we are *only* one by mistake, divorce, or death.

So here I am, a single, waving my list of grievances to signal a great awakening of the married population only to realize *I'm* the one who has been asleep because *I'm* the one who has *allowed* society to define singleness. Their definition of single is "unmarried" . . . the negative side of an expected norm. "Un" is a prefix meaning not. I am *not* married. I should be, but I'm not. If I live by that definition of singleness, I probably live other "un's": UNhappy, UNcertain, UNsettled, UNneeded, UNloved.

Perhaps some of our single frustrations come when we try to put two definitions into the same life-space: the single *one* and the single *un*.

Genesis 36 suggests a solution to one space problem. The families of Jacob and Esau, reunited after their extended estrangement, were living as neighbors now. Although far from equalling the star population, Abraham's promised multiplication continued. But the multiplication process worked two ways. As people and animals multiplied, so did the need for space. Shortages developed. "Their riches were more than that they might dwell together" (Gen. 36:7).

In the interest of harmony and good harvest and home space, Esau moved.

In the interest of happiness and wholeness and positive self-concept, the *un's* have to go. There seems no other way to resolve the incompatibility.

What does being single mean?

It makes a difference how I define singleness. If something has to be wrong with me because I am single, my self-concept suffers. If my self-concept suffers, so does the motivation to develop my potential as one person. Being less than I can be makes me "un."

It makes a difference how I define singleness because it can affect my God-concept. If God does not withhold good things from His children and marriage is a good thing, does that mean I am disinherited? If God promises to give me the desires of my heart, am I living an endurance game? And how does the gift-giving father image fit with the emptiness I feel on a lonely night?

An unhealthy single attitude breeds inequity between head knowledge and living experience. What I know about God must make a difference in the way I live out my singleness. It must reflect the goodness and giving Spirit of God while emphasizing God's perfect choices and desire to make His will easy to know.

There *is* more to being one than being un. There is discovery about one-concepts that give balanced perspective to self-image and God-image. Discovery is the key word. It indicates a process. It implies the possibility of obstacles. It predicts important findings.

To become a discoverer, a person does more than join a club and carry an identification card. He goes on a journey with his eyes wide open. He finds things that other people have not found. For example, we give Columbus credit for *discovering* America when the Indians knew it was here all the time. Why? Because Europe didn't know. To them it was a world-expanding discovery.

We need to make some world-expanding discoveries

that will help us live more one than un. The discovery tools are inexpensive but not necessarily simple: being honest with ourselves, spending more listening time with God, believing that God means what He says, and admitting that any inconsistencies are in ourselves.

Sometimes I must dig through *"uns"* in order to discover important *one* concepts. Often it means I must stop asking "why" questions in order to hear answers. Other times I must realize that people who try to neatly miter life's corners may oversimplify.

For example, I was always told that there were three major decisions that would influence my life:

1. My decision about God,
2. My decision about a career,
3. My decision about a mate.

Two of them I have already made. One is still pending. My well-meaning counsellors stated the last decision as a choice among choices. And for me, any element of choice has been frustratingly out of my hands.

Of course there was Roger. All I did was smile at him from my office desk. It was just a "HowareyoutodayI'mglad" smile. Maybe my eyes squinted more than usual. If they did I was just tired. Fifty-year-old Roger thought I smiled a "Ithinkitwouldbeagoodideaifwegotmarried" smile. He acted on his understanding with a knock on my door later that evening. Never has such a short courtship led to a marriage proposal! If persistence always bred success, once-smiled-at Roger would not be single . . . nor for that matter, would I.

Then there are those times when absent choices are as unsettling as mismatched ones. Consider my journal entry for 12-13-75.

I keep waiting for my knight in shining armor,
But I think there must have been a shortage
—of armor, I mean.

12

Somewhere in our economy crunch
We have had to melt shining armor.
Maybe I just haven't recognized him
Outside of molded iron!

Whether it is because of limited choices or invisible ones, bruised single attitudes come from being out of control.

You have heard of situation ethics? Share my discovery about situation contentment. Paul introduced it: "I have learned the secret of contentment in every situation" (Phil. 4:12). This is the secret of happiness.

There are two meanings for "secret." One is information shared with a selected few. These secrets are called gossip. The other definition is information beyond ordinary understanding. Paul's secret was not the gossip kind. It was the beyond-understanding kind.

I can just see Paul peering through the iron bars of his stone-slab world to share his secret. Something about that contrast makes it a beyond-my-understanding secret. He didn't give credit to the drips and the musty smell and the uninvited rodents for his discovery. He testified to contentment, not of his struggle to find it. In the same way, I don't have to find contentment by struggling through feelings of un-ness, even though sometimes I try.

It is easy enough to shut the world away. Locked doors can do it, or unanswered phones, or smiles you wear only for decoration. Have you been there? I have.

I can hear someone say (for I have been there myself): "I'm not happy. I feel squeezed by a schedule and responsibility that I don't want and don't like. I can't go on like this. There's got to be a way out."

Paul tells me: "No, there's a way in . . . in-the-middle-of. But it's a secret. Something you may not understand right away."

He was right. I didn't.

13

I keep something above my desk to remind me that:
Contentment is not the fulfillment of what you want but the realization of how much you already have.

My "went" list is usually different from my "have" list. When I focus on the difference *between,* I expose gaps that wishful thinking will not fill. If I try to bridge the gaps with an in-spite-of attitude, I create unnecessary struggle. You see, any struggle to find contentment is not *because of* my situation be it single, liberated, married, widowed, or divorced. The struggle comes because *I* chose to view my situation as less than what I want. That's not God's decision. That's mine.

Something else is true. My "have" list is usually longer than my "want" list.

I HAVE:
A worthwhile job
A liveable income
A loving family
A comfortable apartment
A meaningful church family
Sensitive friends
An ever-present, always-giving God
Innumerable promises from God
    about life, liberty, and the pursuit
    of happiness (i.e., contentment)
Writing ability
Speaking opportunities
Personal ministry

Need I continue?

WHAT I WANT:
Fewer job frustrations
More money for less on-the-job time
My own husband and children
More time to write

14

See what I mean? The "haves" *have* it. Working against what I have will not produce what I want. So I explore what I have.

I found one of the most important "haves" while reading 1 Corinthians. It came like a belated Christmas gift one New Year's Eve. I chose to celebrate the calendar change alone.

I occupy the guest room when I am home. The lavender blush softened by the bedside light warmed the stillness. Snuggled beneath Grandma-quilts, I felt cocooned. I journalized a bit, capturing word pictures of my lived-out year. Then I turned to God's Word. First Corinthians 3:22 gave firecracker brilliance to my New Year:

He has given you all of the present and all of the future.
All are yours.

I realized I would need to find the secret of contentment to experience the fullness of that gift.

I am glad Paul was not selfish with his secret. He shared it in hopes that we would also become sharers. What is the secret of situation contentment that allows me to make use of all the today He has given so that I may also enjoy all of tomorrow?

1. *Fix my thoughts on what is true and good and right*
There are good things happening to me right now. That is reality. That is truth. I must focus my attention there. I must put my emotional energy to work with what I *have* instead of dreaming about what I *want*.

2. *Think about those things that are pure and lovely*
My mind works like an impersonal computer. I get out of it exactly what I put into it. If I look at my situation through dark glasses, a dark situation is what I see.

3. *Dwell on the fine, good things in others*
What are the good words about the people in my world? Do I have only good words?

4. *Think about all I can praise God for and be glad about*

What a waste if in my dreams for tomorrow, all of today—all of the praiseworthy things of today, all of the happiness-producing, contentment-filling gifts of God, found only in today—are lost because my thoughts are elsewhere.

Do you see where I am heading? There are far more riches here than most of us imagine—which we lose when we allow "un-ness" to invade our lives. There is more to being one than being un.

God does not cheat me out of any loving gift because I'm single. But I can cheat myself when I allow a negative response to my situation.

And I have. I've sat at home alone on weekends more times than I care to tally. I've been on blind dates, been willing prey to matchmaking schemes . . . only to find dead ends. I came through a four-year courtship and broken engagement. And there are times when I say to myself, If I have to go to one more function unescorted, I just won't go.

I know what it is to be single from several perspectives: the good, the bad, and the almost-not. In the deepest part of my heart, I want to know the happiness a Christian marriage can produce. But I don't want to throw away today for a might-not-happen tomorrow. If I do, I've destroyed the only bridge to my future.

The saddest thing that could happen to me is not to spend my life single . . . it would be to miss what God wills or act unwillingly toward it. It would be to look in retrospect from married life and wish I were single so I could appreciate all that I missed.

Am I only one? I don't have to be. I can be more than that because *there is more to being one than being un.*

There is discovery. There is an unending "have" list. There is the secret of situation contentment. There is the desire to be all that God intends for me to be. And that single-minded attitude opens myself to God's double exposure to abundant life:

> *Now glory be to God*
> *Who by his mighty power at work within us*
> *Is able to do far more than we would dare*
> > *to ask*
> > *or even dream of—*
> > *infinitely beyond*
> > *our highest prayers*
> > > *desires*
> > > *thoughts*
> > > *hopes.* —Eph. 3:20

May I pray for you . . . and me?

> *O God,*
> *Sift through our single-minded attitudes.*
> *Where there is buried treasure,*
> > *Help us become discoverers with newly opened*
> > *eyes.*
> *Where we hold our tear-smudged "want" lists,*
> > *Help us appreciate all we already have.*
> *Where there is struggle,*
> > *Help us learn the secret to situation contentment.*
> *Lead us to New Year resolution*
> *Through Your life-in-us abundance;*
> *And we will once again*
> *Be ready for today,*
> *Realizing we can trust*
> > *Your timing*
> > *Your plan*
> > *Your love.*
> > > *Amen!*

17

Introduction to Growth Designs

Outside my second-floor apartment is a field. Not too long ago only weeds grew there. Waist-high, the chaotic growth looked like nobody cared . . . because nobody did! Then one day the old growth was plowed and turned into the earth. Newly furrowed soil prepared to conceive and reproduce. First it was corn. Another time it was wheat. What made the difference between weed-growth and good-growth? A plan. A design.

Unheeded, my life will grow weeds. Self-destructive attitudes. Negative tomorrow feelings. Discontent. Fear. Loneliness. God has a better design. It is one that cultivates order and wholeness and positive self concepts. However, they don't grow by accident. They must be planned.

At the end of each chapter of this book there is a growth design. It includes a series of what-does-this-mean-to-me questions based on chapter concepts. It ends with immediate application ideas to help you begin growing. Keep a notebook handy in which to write your answers and/or responses.

Consider the fact that it takes approximately 30 to 60 days to change a habit, especially an attitude habit. Therefore, don't expect overnight changes. Also remember that *very* small, sure-to-succeed-at goals result in positive feelings about growing. It also generates motivation to grow more.

Perhaps you will want to make this book the thrust of a small-group study. One important advantage in following this method is the accountability factor involved. Verbalizing your awareness of a growth need can offset self-discipline weaknesses. It also means that a group of people who believe in you and God's ability to help you grow, are praying for you.

Whether you complete the growth designs by yourself or in a small group, review your growth goals each day. And pray. For awareness. First steps. Right direction.

This is my prayer for growth. I hope you will make it yours:

Dear God
Of the Good Earth
   where planted seeds
   bear fruit in due season;
Touch me with Your growth.
Where my life is weed-thick
   with tangled roots
Or desert-dry
   with sparse growth,
Make me aware of your design for growing.
Help me see that Your cycle of
   plowing
     seeding
       watering
        weeding

> *Is the way to harvest growth*
> *In my life too.*
>
> *Increase awareness*
> *Of my need to grow.*
> *Supply the energy*
> *To step into growth*
>   *as slowly*
>   *as insures success*
>   *as steady*
>   *as discipleship demands*
> *So that I*
> *Will always*
> *Be growing up*
> *In You.*

GROWTH DESIGN

1. More than Un

What "uns" are you aware of in your life?

Galatians 5:22 promises more than un-ness.
According to this verse, the key to being more than "un" is:

2. Discovery Practice

Be honest

    What is your biggest dream? frustration? happiness? question? Talk to God about it. Then ask

Him to help you release your emotional hold on it in a way that allows Him to speak and guide.

Be still

Close your eyes and personalize Ps. 46:10. *Help me to be still so that I can know You are God.* How does knowing He is God affect "un" areas of your life?

Believe

Be secure in the fact that what God wants you to know, He will communicate to an open, sensitive, searching heart.

3. Sharing Secrets with Paul

Take a reality picture (Phil. 4:8)

Make a list of what you *have.* Compare it with what you *want.* Summarize your discovery.
Repeat the definition of contentment.
Where is the key to your contentment?

Take a beauty break

Walk in a park. Look out a window. Admire the sleek lines of a new car. Spend time with someone whose beautiful spirit is contagious. Let heaven fill your thoughts!

Take time to compliment

Who needs your good words? Be generous with them. Plan to plant a compliment in every conversation you have.

Take time to praise

Write your praise in a poem or prayer.
Sing your praise, or hum, or whistle.
Share your praiseworthy blessings with others.
Read one of David's praise-songs, like Psalm 139. Personalize it.

GROWTH DESIGN

Where I need to grow:

How I will know when I have grown:

What I plan to *do* today:

Chapter Two

Beginning with One

My three-year-old niece is learning to count. It is still a memory game for her. On some days she jumps out of bed by 1-2-3 but other times she puts blocks away by 1-3-5-4. She may confuse the order but she never misses the starting point.

It makes a difference where you begin. Try eating the middle peppermint scoop from a three-dip cone. Try starting a book at chapter 15. Try driving a car without turning on the ignition.

Wrong beginnings make progress difficult. More specifically for singles, un-ness may develop from missing the right starting point.

I thought my problem was not having *someone.* I guess it wouldn't bother me so much if God would just take away my expectation for hoped-for love. Just tell me I will never marry. I think I could take that . . . a settlement. But this gray area creates limbo. I live with an if-I-marry clause that designs either/or possibilities and a temporary feeling about life.

I dreamed that love and marriage would take away

lonely weekends, insurance frustration, tax enigmas, and car confusion. I would decorate a dream apartment, produce gourmet meals by candlelight, and be picture-perfect for my husband's eyes.

Of course, that is a female reaction, but the other side is just as soap-opera. Someone to cook what I like: meat and potatoes. Laundry kept up to date. Live-in pickup service. Arms around me when I feel like loving. Understanding distance when I don't.

Where do those dreams take me? Away from the beginning. Away from me and what I have. And the more time I spend on the wrong first step, the more frustration I find in irresolution.

I'm not sure when I realized what I was doing. But somewhere in my single pilgrimage, God began to shine new light on my oneness.

To count, begin with one. In the beginning there was *one* God. In the beginning God created *one* man. (Have you ever thought about Adam's introduction to this world as a single person . . . short-lived though it may have been?)

Beginning with what might happen tomorrow is skipping the all-important first step. The easiest way to do this is to play "if only" games.

The object is to identify a scapegoat for any un-ness present in my life. It goes like this: I award myself one frustration point per if-only statement. When playing with a group of people, award bonus points if I receive sympathy for my if-only statement.

The irony is that the one with the most points . . . loses.

Look at three sample rounds. Have you ever played . . .

24

1. *If Only Someone Loved Me, I Would Love Myself*

Dr. Bell is a professor of psychology. He told me of a girl who wanted more than anything else to be married. She was sure that if she were just married, she would be happier. She had asked God over and over again why he had not sent someone.

"Suppose God gave you what you wanted today?" Dr. Bell asked. "Suppose he sent your prince charming your way. Would you be able to be a wife that could satisfy him the way you presently feel about yourself?"

She looked down.

"No."

He went on to tell me:

"For some, marriage is a way of not facing up to the problems of the single individual. It is an escape from themselves. They seem to be saying, 'I will like myself better if someone else likes me.' They want to be rescued . . . by marriage. But if they have not found themselves as single individuals, marriage only makes the discovery more difficult and, for some, impossible. For them, marriage is an extension of their fantasy world and the reality of marriage is a disappointment."

I know of no married couples who have never been single, but I know of many married couples, who because they neglected some of the important steps in being single, are having trouble in marriage. It makes a difference where I start.

2. *If Only I Were Married I Would Be More Spiritually Mature*

He was single, a college graduate, already successful in an at-least-for-now career. His polished smile and in-control authority both uneased and relaxed me. Behind his wide-eyed welcome to the retreat, was friendship.

25

Throughout the weekend, his questions revealed his stretch for truth.

"I really want a day-to-day Bible study and prayer pattern. But sometimes my self-discipline is weak. It just seems that if I were married, it would be easier to study and grow together. Sometimes I am afraid I won't be the mature Christian I should be until I marry."

He is not alone in this feeling. Others of us have read with envy the Laymen's Retreat emphasis upon marriage enrichment through spiritual growth. "If only I were married, I would go and learn how to grow as a Christian. It just seems like marriage provides an obvious proving ground for lessons. Not to mention mutual encouragement."

But it is our narrow perspective and wrong beginning that is the real problem. Roommates can provide proving ground and mutual encouragement as can co-workers, and family and anyone in the Body of Christ.

I know of no one who is spiritually perfect, single or married. But I know a lot of people who are having difficulty getting even close because of if-only rationalizations. It makes a difference where I begin addressing the problem.

3. *If Only I Had a Better Job*

I was cutting up a tossed salad one evening and almost added the tip of my finger. What good was my college education if it didn't place me in a job that combined my interest and my ability, I thought as I attacked the cucumber. How long would I be compelled to live within walking distance to everything because I couldn't afford a car? (And I sliced the tomato with the dull edge of the knife squishing tomato juice everywhere.) If only I had a better job, I would be happy. I would be motivated to improve myself. I would be fulfilled.

I spend 40 hours a week or more working at a job that has the power to manipulate my emotional equilibrium. If work goes well, it is a good day. But if the Xerox machine eats my 10-page original, if the boss schedules an unscheduled meeting, if the janitor empties a box of files instead of the trash can, or if my ball-point pen runs out of ball-point, the world is coming to an end and I'm a failure.

It makes a difference where I place blame. Since then, I have learned that with a *better* job comes more complex problems. With a *better* job I work more than 40 hours a week. And with a *better* job . . . I want a *better* job!

In a society where experience is focal, I know of no one who starts at the top, except by inheritance. However, I know a lot of people who, because they wasted ground-level experience, never advanced very far.

I have drooled over if-only clothes. (I would buy them if-only I had someone to impress!) I have neglected if-only entertainment. (I would go if-only I had someone to go with me.) I have daydreamed chapters of if-only life. (It would happen if-only I were someone else.)

I faced my backward spiral one afternoon on the way to substitute teach in an adult education speech class.

I grabbed a slice of cold meat loaf, changed clothes, and locked myself in my car for the drive to Watseka. I left papers to grade, schedules to make out, midterms to average. I think I *needed* to leave those things . . . for a while.

The road was uncrowded and I tried to allow the open space to uncrowd my mind and emotions. As I soaked in the silence, I began to talk to God . . . out loud. He already knew everything I was thinking, but I'm not so sure I did. It was good for me to hear our conversation.

I remember a long-ago question: When you look in the mirror, what do you see . . . everything that is right with yourself or everything that is wrong? That day I saw everything that was wrong and blamed all the wrong reasons.

Then there were tears. Not tired tears. Tears that came from discovering inequality again: Who I am now and who I want to be.

I gave myself to God again. Not only the surrender of life and will. I gave my clothes and my hair and my complexion and my fingernails. I asked him to help me develop the feminine qualities of charm, grace, poise, and beauty. I realized anew that if I wanted to become the person of my potential, I had to start now . . . not tomorrow when I fall in love or tomorrow when I make more money or tomorrow when I have fewer problems.

The counting process begins with one and the time is NOW. Go back to the beginning The first step is me. Of course, I am not recommending a me-first ego trip. However, I am suggesting that if the expression of my self-concept helps me to be all the person that I can be now . . . while I am single . . . then I know I am not building my life on dreams and prince charmings and fairytale romance.

If I can't handle problems like loneliness, depression, and job frustration while I am single, adding another person's loneliness, depression, and job frustration won't make it any easier. Simple arithmetic tells me that.

Although being single is definitely the first step, it does not necessarily mean that marriage is the second. Statistics confirm that we will not all live two-by-two. With 25,000 single females and 18,000 single males, not everyone will marry or remarry.

Therefore it is to the advantage of my emotional well-being to consider singleness as more than just a waiting room for marriage. It is an important part of my development as a person. It is a time in my life that allows me to know who I am by myself. It is a time that invites me to like myself . . . all by myself.

But how do I begin? How long do I have to hurt before good starts happening? How long do I have to struggle with the way things are before they change? If the best is yet to be, when does it start getting better?

Have you ever asked those questions? They don't come just from being single. They come when we find ourselves living in the no-man's (or woman's)-land between God's promised good and obstacles that seem to prevent it.

That's where the children of Israel lived. God promised a safe, bountiful land. But they spent 400 years in slavery and 40 years in the wilderness before ultimately possessing the land promised to Father Abraham. Exodus through Deuteronomy presents a summary of a God-protected people getting ready to receive good gifts. In it, I find four beginning principles that apply to wilderness walks as well as promised-land possession.

1. *I Begin by Getting Rid of Slavery* (Exod. 13:3)

Of course no one has me in chains, but sometimes my apartment imprisons me. Sometimes I am a slave to my own ideas: how *I* think my single life should be designed, or how long *I* think I should be single.

As long as the children of Israel were slaves in Egypt, they couldn't get to Canaan. First they had to get rid of the bonds that kept them from going where they should go and being who they should be.

As long as I am tied to limited thinking, God cannot lead me into His unlimited life.

2. *I Begin by Realizing the Most Direct Route Is Not Always the Best Way* (Exod. 13:17)

Sometimes I feel like a detour sign is saying: This is

just to make it hard for you. But that's not it at all. The way is closed because of obstacles I may not see. In thoughtfulness for the drivers, a detour sign suggests a better route.

God led the children of Israel the long way around via Sinai on purpose. It wasn't just to make it more difficult. It was because taking the shortest way directly northward held great hazards that only God could see (Exod. 13:17-18). Besides, God needed to get the Israelites organized, give them their laws, and establish their worship before they headed for the Promised Land. Even the unwanted wilderness wanderings taught them needed lessons concerning dependence upon God.

There is a good reason why we don't take an as-the-crow-flies route in our lives . . . we can't fly.

3. *I Begin by Learning to Follow His Signs* (Exod. 13:21-22)

What good are signs if you can't find them? Have you ever looked for a house on an unlighted street where the numbers were stenciled on the curb or inscribed on a four-inch doorpost?

Knowing how to read signs is just as important. One time on a trip I looked for a place to spend the night after reaching my driving threshhold. The sign advertising a Howard Johnson's just off the highway was large enough for anyone to see. "Just Ahead" it said. Within the quarter mile, I saw it and took the next exit ramp only to find myself on the wrong access road. When I backtracked to read the sign again, I saw for the first time: "Take the Linwood Boulevard exit *before* Howard Johnson's."

God made it possible for the Israelites to follow tangible signs. He made His way easy to see: an unmistakable cloud by day, an irrefutable blaze by night.

Where do we get the idea that discovering God's way

is a guessing game? God gives us signs as bold as an angel-light proclamation, as definite as a guiding star. Peace is one of His signs: "Where the Spirit of the Lord is, there is peace," the song says, implying if the peace isn't there, you are in the wrong receiving line. Joy is one of His signs. Not just a smiling mask but in-the-middle-of-anywhere joy.

God doesn't hide His signs on unlighted streets or in bottom-line fine print. He shares them all . . . in His Word. "Know what his Word says and means" (2 Tim. 2:15). It is the only way to learn His sign language.

4. *I Begin by Learning to Obey*

My gas gauge read empty. *But my car is good for at least 10 more miles. Besides, I just have to go a couple of blocks. I'll get gas on my way home.* I had forgotten how many days I had been saying that. Unfortunately, my car had an elephant's memory. According to her calculations, I had said it for the last time. That evening, I was actually on my way to get gas when she coughed and sputtered and went into a coma.

We are like children when our lessons in obedience are learned by trial and error.

Over and over again, the word "obey" is repeated from Exodus through Deuteronomy. That's all they had to do: follow the leader, obey instructions, pay attention to the signs. You would think that after the Red Sea miracle and water from rocks and manna from heaven, the Israelites would realize the advantages of obedience.

However, when they became irritable because there was no food or water, they questioned. When they were tired of not being able to see God, they built an idol. When they thought Moses was just being fastidious about picking up all the manna that fell, they ended up with smelly maggots the next day.

31

God desires our obedience because it puts us in a direct receiving line for His good gifts. He promises success if we obey (Josh. 1:7). He promises to reveal himself to those who obey (John 14:23). He shares his friendship with those who obey (John 15:15). I don't have to see the future or understand the present. That is God's role in my life. I just have to listen carefully to all He says to me and to obey. It is for my own good (Deut. 10:12).

The right beginning requires the right first step. Let me say it again, the difference between un-ness and one-ness is where I start. The difference can be eliminated when I start with who I am and Who is at work within me.

"God will make you the kind of children he wants to have—will make you as good as you wish you could be!" (2 Thess. 1:11). Of course, I have to be careful how I interpret the word "good." I can't count on free plastic surgery to remake my physical features. However, He does promise His help "for each day's problems" (Col. 2:6c). By living "in vital union with him" (Col. 2:6d), I can subtract worry lines and replace them with the common denominator of all handsomeness and beauty . . . a smile. I can't expect a promotion in the morning, but I can expect God to help me "enjoy [my] work and accept [my] lot in life." Eccles. 5:19 says it is God's gift to me.

So the first step is focusing on who I am and what I have. It is the matter of situation contentment again. The if-only-I-were-married syndrome only digs depression holes that marriage may not fill. If-only focuses on what I don't have. God wants us "to give what [we] have, not what [we] haven't" (2 Cor. 8:12).

Besides, if I use well what God has given me now, there is wonderful joy ahead (1 Pet. 1:6). *"The man who uses well what he is given shall be given more and he shall have abundance. But from the man who is unfaithful, even*

32

what little responsibility he has shall be taken from him"
(Matt. 25:29).

It has been a life-changing lesson for me to learn the difference between a tithe and stewardship. Tithe is just one-tenth; but stewardship is taking care of everything God has given me. Stewardship should be the qualifying characteristic of a truly Christian life-style.

Too often we compare life to a vertical climb without applying the most elemental management principle. In the vertical climb in the business world, big jobs give way to bigger jobs . . . but not until the big job is successfully completed. The lessons a junior executive learns, the senior executive must already have learned. If by faulty evaluation of a person's ability, promotion is premature, there is a responsibility overload. If the person is unable to close the gap, there may be painful and debilitating failure.

Sometimes I have had to learn the hard way that when there is a series of steps involved, order is important. For example, it has taken me a long time to learn how to make un-lumpy sauces. I remember my first lemon meringue pie. I melted the butter, added the lemon juice and sugar, then dumped in the cornstarch. As the mixture began to heat, I noticed lumps I could not stir out. I had forgotten an important step. If I don't separate the cornstarch grains before heating, the heat penetrates unevenly and the result . . . Lemon Dumpling Meringue Pie (which is no one's favorite dessert).

There are steps, and order is important.

Once a man who skipped a step met Jesus. He was a rich man as men counted riches—by camels and servants and gold coins jingling in a money pouch. He was a religious man as men judged religion by rules and sacrifices and synogogue attendance.

"What can I do?" said the rich man who had already spent his life doing good things in the wrong order.

"Love," Jesus replied, "by honoring God, life, marriage, property, honesty, parents, friendship, and yourself."

"But that's what I do," the rich man answered, revealing his lack of understanding.

"Then demonstrate your love priority by selling everything you have to help the poor."

The rich man could not part with his possessions, because he did not love God wholly first. He had skipped a step.

Jesus grieves for people who skip steps. They are not always timesavers. In fact, people who skip steps sometimes waste entire lives.

I'm not interested in wasting my life, single or married. I want to find out how one is more than un, because I will always be one person. So I ask God to help me begin with the one that I am. It is a first step marked by the understanding that, "as I yield myself more fully to God, he expresses his plan more perfectly in me," to quote Glenn Clark. I ask Him to order the steps in my life so I won't skip any necessary part of my development. I ask Him to use His creative power, to make new where I hold on to if-only dreams, negative self-concepts, and narrow perspective.

There is more to being one than being un. Being one is a beginning.

In the beginning, "God began creating" (Gen. 1:1). This says to me that if we allow Him, He still creates.

Let's ask Him to.

God,
You know where I am in my life.

34

You know where I feel
   more endings
   than beginnings.
You know where I am more aware of
   who I am not
   than who I am.
You
Who created
   light out of darkness
   form out of void
   life out of the inanimate
Create meaning and fulfillment in me.
Continue to reveal the all-important steps
   that I must not skip as I seek
   to develop as Your child.
Keep my eyes and heart fixed
   not just on the promise of tomorrow
But on being the most creative person
In my today.
AMEN!

Growth Design

1. If Only

Write down an "if-only" statement you have been using.

Circle the "if-only" clause.

Read Rom. 8:31. Circle the "if" clause from that scripture.

What difference in dependence is there between the two "if" statements?

Rewrite *your* if-only clause. How can you change the dependency factor in your life?

35

2. The Chain Gang

A chain is an idea or situation that prevents your freedom to *do* and to *be* your potential.

What is an example of a chain in your life?
If you believe John 8:32, what truth is God wanting to communicate to you?

3. Detours

What detours have frustrated you in your life?
Read Jeremiah 29:11.
What life attitudes demonstrate a belief in God's protective guidance?

How can you incorporate these attitudes into your life?

4. Sign Language

Fill in this chart after reading the reference:

Ref.	*God's sign is:*	*I experience it as I:*
Isa. 26:3		
Rom. 5:13		
Prov. 29:25		
Ps. 25:4-5, 8-10		

5. Learning to Obey

Read Deut. 11:1-32
How many times is the word "obey" used?
What rewards belong to God's obedient children?
What punishment?
In what area of my life do I need to practice immediate obedience?

6. In Focus

Focus on who I am

How can you begin to enjoy all of who you are and where you are?

by teaching someone the hobby you enjoy?
by using one of your strengths to help someone?
by making a new purchase for your house/car?
by inviting friends over for popcorn and games?
by _____?

Focus on what I have

As stewardship means "using well what God has given," where do I need to give some special attention?

How am I *using well:*

my apartment?
my car?
my single life?
my family?
my church membership?
the promises God has given?

Focus on right order

Read Ps. 37:23.

Write a prayer that expresses to God how you are willing to allow Him complete freedom to create order in your life.

GROWTH DESIGN

Where I need to grow:

How I will know when I have grown:

What I plan to *do* today:

Chapter Three

Selected by One

I remember playing Red Rover in grade school. I think it was the first tomboy influence in my life. Most of the time my near-arm-breaking attack gave me the honor of being captain of the team the next day. As captain, it was my responsibility to choose my team.

Being an every-time-we-played surviving veteran of the game, I had ranked all possible recruits. There were the *bruisers*. They aim for the fleshy forearm. With their hands clasped at their waist, they attack with the streamlined point of a rocket. Then there were the *bulldozers*. With face viciously contorted, knuckles whitened by tight clench, and a guttural grunt—much like that of a stalking wolf—this Red-Roving romper built momentum immediately and demolished any obstacle in his path . . . just like a bulldozer. Last, and certainly least, were the *bouncers*. These were usually fraidycat girls who bounded into the human hedge only to be bounced off.

Of course a good team balanced the offence with defense, and I knew who were strong chains and weak links. Personally, I thought my record of choosing was unbeatable. But sometimes my classmates made a coming-up-in-the-ranks achiever the Captain's Choice.

Of course there is more to life than choosing all-star Red Rover teams, but there are times when choices make or bruise us.

Have you ever gone into Baskin-Robbins and tried to choose one flavor from their 32 taste-tickling delights? You probably ended up like me, with a three-dip cone, each dip a different flavor, and that's not counting the five flavors you pretested with a mini-spoon.

Well, life isn't an ice-cream store either, even if we sometimes order more than we can comfortably handle.

But life does require choices. And sometimes it means one-choices. *There is more to being one than being un . . .* there is selection.

I know what you are thinking. "Wait just one minute. If you think I'm single because I have chosen it, you're wrong." All right, but stay with me until you understand what I am saying.

Some time before Thanksgiving my family begins to talk about Christmas. With glints in their eyes and a practiced nonchalance in their voices, they drop subtle hints, "You know what I need . . . You know what I wish I had . . .?" Then at our Thanksgiving reunion, our "want" lists are due.

A "want" list is the logical solution to what to buy for the family member you see only once or twice a year. It may list possible wardrobe additions, indicate worn-out necessities, or enlighten about hoped-for luxuries.

My automobile mechanic, mountain-climbing, scuba-diving, parachuting brother's list is the most complete. He itemizes 20 to 30 suggestions, giving catalog page number, price, store, and directions to get there.

But I like surprises, so you know what I usually do? Even before the Christmas wrapping paper has been shelved for another year, I begin prying for Christmas gift ideas. Then when next Christmas comes I take out those "want" lists to confirm my ideas that are *not* listed.

Isn't that ridiculous? Or is it? Doesn't that just emphasize my strong desire to make personal selections? After all, even though my family makes suggestions, I am the giver. I make the final choice.

No one questions the giver's ultimate responsibility of selection at Christmas. However, when it comes to life-gifts, we sometimes forget that the privilege of selection still remains with God, the Ultimate Giver.

James 1:17 tells us that God is a giver of good gifts: "Whatever is good and perfect comes to us from God." Psalm 40:4 reminds us that "many blessings are given to those who trust the Lord." Then the best way to utilize His good gifts is with my yielded life.

There is an important reason why I can trust God's selections for my life. Verse by verse Psalm 139 pointedly tells me that God's expertise as a Giver of good gifts is based on His personal knowledge about me. He knows the ratio between my ability and my productivity. He sees the long-range results of reached-for goals and the short-range, progress-marking steps that take me there. He knows my strengths and weaknesses and how to balance them successfully. Fleeting thoughts or whispered prayers do not escape Him. His all-seeing eye prepares the future. His shepherd's heart guides the way.

God's omniscience is not just a theological characteristic to be studied. It affects my day-to-day life. He always knows me better than my parents, my best friend, or a mate. I can be comfortable and secure in His knowledge about me because He uses that knowledge to select good gifts.

Do you see where I am leading? If I believe I am following God's will for my life . . . *and I do;* if I believe that

41

God uses His intimate knowledge about me only to help me . . . *and I do;* and if I believe that nothing outside of my own rejection and disobedience can separate me from God's love and His good things . . . *and I really do;* then I must accept being single as a part of God's plan for my life at this time. I haven't necessarily selected it. God has. I am not the selector. God is.

Too often we allow our perspective of our environment to distort the prospects of enjoying God's good gifts.

If ever a people lived under environmental limitations, the Hebrew children did: plagues, Red Sea, wilderness, captivity. However, God continued to promise good gifts and gave instructions in how to receive them.

During one period of Israel's disobedience, Jeremiah had urged their repentance and predicted their enslavement. False prophets had been the source of disunity. Some Israelites even began to reject the idea of a "chosen people." After all, if this was the way He treated His "chosen"; how did He treat the "left-out"? But now reality confirmed Jeremiah's words. They were captives of Babylonia, just like he had prophesied. Freedom was 70 years away.

It would have been easy for Jeremiah to gloat with an "I-told-you-so" arrogance. Instead, aware of Jerusalem's confusion and fear of the future, Jeremiah sent a letter that God dictated. Basically, it gave getting-on-with-your-life instructions. Then in Jer. 29:11, God reminds us all who is the Giver . . . and why: "For I know the plans I have for you, says the Lord. They are plans for good and not for evil, to give you a future and a hope."

What does it say about God's control in my life if I reject part of His specific plan? What does it say about my confidence in His good gifts if I run myself in circles asking "Why?" Somehow there needs to be a close coordination between my mental-verbal acceptance and my attitude-action response.

Whenever I am faced with a situation I did not specifically ask for but desire to find God's goodness in, I re-read Rom. 5:2: "For because of our faith, he has brought us into this place of highest privilege where we now stand, and we confidently and joyfully look forward to actually becoming all that God has in mind for us to be."

Now I do not use this verse to say that because of my faith-walk with God I am here, single. Nor am I trying to construct a comparison between being married and being single to prove that "the greatest of these" is being single (even if Paul might not have objected to that paraphrase).

This verse goes past any specific situation description. It is faith, that hoped-for substance, the evidence of unseen reality, that helps me enjoy God's good gifts. It is faith, not status or a lack of it, beauty or plainness, personality or peculiarity.

And because I have faith in God's goodness to me, I always enjoy a place of highest privilege. However, it is not a matter of being happily married or painfully widowed, freely single or uncomfortably divorced. The place of highest privilege is a place of accepting God's good gifts.

Some of us reject privileges because we do not accept them.

On his way home from school every day, a little boy with empty pockets, passed a candy store. As he pressed his face against the window, he could almost taste the rich chocolate or nutty squares or multi-colored fruit-flavored drops. Inside the store, the ring of the cash register indicated someone would soon savor these confections. Always, just as the little boy lifted his eyes from the candy into the shop, the store clerk smiled and beckoned him in. Each time, the little boy remembered his empty pockets, and ran away.

One day, the little boy found a quarter on the sidewalk. "Now I can buy some candy," he thought. When he came to the candy store, he examined the window display in order to make his selection. When he looked up, there was the store clerk, smiling and inviting him inside. This time he accepted, with his hand inside his pocket, protecting his newfound "candy" money.

"Hi, son!" greeted the smiling store clerk. "You know, when I first saw you outside my window, I said, 'Now there's a true candy-lover if I ever saw one.'"

But the little boy was too taken up with just being inside the store to hear the clerk. Inside he not only could see more candy choices, but he could smell it as well. It made him wish that there was one super-special candy bar that mixed all the candy together.

"Yes, I knew the first time I saw you," the man continued. "And I said to myself, 'I bet he likes chocolate best of all.' So I've been saving this special chocolate bar just for you."

Now the little boy looked at the man who was trying to give him a piece of candy that was bigger than any of the pieces in the display windows. All he had to do was take it. So he did.

"I would have given it to you earlier, but you always ran away," the man said.

And the little boy went home with a chocolate bar in one hand and a quarter in his pocket . . . for tomorrow.

How many times have glass windows and empty pockets prevented our accepting what God wants to give us? We struggle through a difficult time, just looking through the window, wishing things were different, wishing we had what it took to "buy" a different set of circum-

44

stances. And God says, "I would have given what you needed earlier, but you always ran away."

The place of highest privilege goes beyond a description of circumstances and vital statistics. It is the place where we initiate hospitality toward God. We accept. We receive.

And through this acceptance, we grow. Through this acceptance we become more of who God meant for us to be: more happy, more optimistic, more peaceful, more mature.

But what if I interrupted God's process of selection for me? What if *my* will superceded *His* will? What if the divorce was a mistake because the marriage should never have happened? What if my college years were spent in rebellion and self-chosen separation from God?

The Bible clearly tells us that there are consequences for sin and breaking fellowship with God: "If [my] children forsake my laws and don't obey them, then I will punish them" (Ps. 89:32).

However, the Light that shines in such darkness illuminates the provision for reunion: *"My little children, I am telling you this so that you will stay away from sin. But if you sin, there is someone to plead for you before the Father. His name is Jesus . . . he is the forgiveness for our sins* (1 John 2:1-2).

Of course, renewing fellowship with God does not mean we can backtrack our lives to remake the past. And the on-goingness of life the way God created it will not allow us the privilege of starting over from scratch. But submitting to God's supremacy does provide a new foundation for continuing. Allowing His will to work for our good does give us a source of wisdom for dealing with present consequences of our past.

The Bible does not substantiate the theory that God's goodness is reserved only for those who have never broken fellowship with God. David is a prime example. How many times did David's will get in the way of God's perfect choice? When David repented, God renewed fellowship. But God did not take away the consequences of the previous wrong choices. At the same time, He did not withhold future good, either. Isaiah reminds Jerusalem of this fact when he shares God's Word: "I am ready to make an everlasting covenant with you, to give you all the unfailing mercies and love that I had for King David" (Isa. 55:3).

How many times does God ask you to repent a wrong action? Just once. How many times must God forgive that wrong for His forgiveness to stick? Just once. Then why don't we follow God's example and forgive ourselves once and let it stick so we can get on with God's good things? It can be the difference between a fearful "What if I had not . . ." and a confident, "Now that God is choosing . . ."

Sometimes I'm glad that people continue to ask, "What's a nice girl like you doing single?" It means they must think my singleness is for some other reason than appearance or personality. At least that attitude lifts a limp ego. But it also makes me look for other reasons . . . not the least of which is the matter of timing. God's clock versus mine. They are not always synchronized.

I understand there is a line of demarcation in every classroom. I have been on both sides. From that double perspective, I understand that the opening-closing bell system carries a different meaning depending on which side of the line you are. It is especially crucial when the closing bell rings and the teacher is still talking. Do you get up to leave or wait to be dismissed? It depends on who is *really* boss.

To answer the question, "Who is *really* boss" in my life, I must do more than repeat the phrase "Jesus is Lord" and raise a pointing finger. A testimony is a matter of personal experience. If I *say* I have submitted to God's control of my life, I must accept His Lordship in the matter of timing—especially as it applies to being single.

The timing problem is not a new one. We have wrestled with it since birth. Last summer, I watched my week-old nephew fight a few rounds with it. His physical needs triggered an alarm system more dependable than GE or Westclox. At least eight times a day, his system sounded. Only a warm bottle quieted the house again.

A problem of synchronization developed if his mother's clock was running one unmixed, unwarmed bottle behind. Kyle vamped several bars of "Feed Me Now!" in painful vibrato until his mother adjusted her clock. He had yet to learn an important constant about life: to receive what you want before it is ready is more distasteful than just wanting.

It is easy to understand why a week-old baby had not learned that lesson. But what about someone who has lived 20, 30, 40 years or more?

A matter of timing. It is involved in most of the frustrating experiences of life. Why *doesn't* it happen? Marriage, a job? Or why is it happening *now?* Loneliness, job pressures, a broken-down car?

Proverbs has a way of hitting me between the eyes when I least expect it. Consider this bull's-eye verse: "Since the Lord is directing our steps, why try to understand everything that happens along the way? (Prov. 20:24).

"Since" is an adverbial conjunction. It connects God's direction to my in-spite-of-not-understanding steps. *Since* God has proved His leadership credentials in every imaginable situation, and *since* He sees the before and after in one look, why do I have to understand? Why shouldn't I trust God with every important and unimportant desire of my heart? Why shouldn't I believe that God's love will express itself to me in ways that will free me of frustration and keep me from destroying my self image? Why should I let questions about time prevent that connection between God's leadership and my following?

If I learn to resolve the time issue during these years, I lay a cement foundation for future stability in times of crisis and unending query. If I can handle the time problem in the matter of being single, I think it will teach me to handle it in other important life situations.

How do I adjust to God's timing? I have to start where I am. If I can't get past asking "Why?" I am not ready to hear His answer. So I pray:

> *Create in me a new spirit:*
> *One that listens and accepts*
> *Rather than asks and argues.*

Then I am ready for the next step: determining a positive response to God's answer of "Wait" or "No" when He doesn't say "Yes." It is more than a matter of taking sugar-coated medicine or the "I-should-like-it-because-it's-good-for-me" spinach attitude. It is a willingness to let God define His good things for me. It is a willingness to let God's good things take time.

When I first started cooking, I learned the hard way that good things take time. I was always in a hurry. Either I had planned too many entrees or allowed too little time. Usually it was both. To rectify the time problem, I turned the fire all the way up on the spaghetti or chili or macaroni and cheese. By the time I checked the item's progress, the inside of the pan appeared to be Teflon coated and that was before Teflon was invented.

Good things take time and quality is worth waiting for. I have to be willing to admit that if I chafe under His timing, it does not uncover flaws in His plan, but my need for further growth. "The person who truly loves God is the one who is open to God's knowledge" (1 Cor. 8:3). When I am ready to *hear* His answer, when I am ready to *respond* positively to it, then I am ready to let the good that this time holds for me, work *for* me and add to my life rather than subtract from it. God has all the time in the world. I don't.

Learning to accept God's sovereignty in my life is more than a *single* lesson. It is for all who desire life in beyond-your-wildest-dreams abundance. When I give God complete freedom to select and I demonstrate my faith in His choices with my unquestioning acceptance, I enjoy single experiences of His design. They are unique because of His intimate knowledge of me. They are surprises when I allow Him to fill in the blanks of my "want" list. They are never-ending because He always wraps plenty into tomorrow. And I never have to be afraid of His plan or time. I have His Word on it.

Let's give Him ours.

> *O God,*
> *I can't pretend*
> *In this moment of truth,*
> *For to be anything but truthful*
> *Before Your all-knowing heart*
> *Is to live*
> > *the most ridiculous*
> > > *and unnecessary lie.*
>
> *Where there is frustration*
> *I want to learn acceptance.*
>
> *Where there is confusion*
> *I want to learn to cease striving*
> *And know that You are God*
> *And You will gladly give*

Your peace re-stilling,
  Joy infilling
  Will.

It is enough
To make each day
A select experience
To explore.

Thank You!

GROWTH DESIGN

1. A Good Giver

Based on the following references, what characteristics describe God's kind of giving?

Jas. 1:1
Ps. 37:4
Ps. 40:4
Matt. 7:11

2. Inside Knowledge

Psalm 139 tells us how much He knows.
List the areas of His inside knowledge:

Rewrite Jer. 29:11 to reflect your reaction to this intimate knowledge.

3. Changing the Question

What "why" questions are frustrating you in your life?
Rewrite them, changing them to "how" questions.

4. The Key Is Acceptance

On a scale of 1-5, where 1 is feeling like a king/queen and 5 is down in the dumps, how would you rate your "privileged state"?

What factors need to change in order to increase that privilege rating?
   a. feelings
   b. job, apartment, single status, etc.
   c. God's selections

Put a plus beside the factors you have control of.

Select one trouble spot with a low privilege rating and direct your prayer in the following way:
   a. Admit the feeling of low privilege or the attitude of nonacceptance.
   b. Thank God for His desire to direct your steps. Admit that it is too much for you to handle.
   c. Think about one of God's good gifts you will experience in the next 24 hours. How can you enjoy it the most?
   d. Is there some way you can apply that kind of enjoyment/acceptance to the trouble spot?

5. A Matter of Timing

Since the Lord is directing, what do I do with my desire to understand?

6. Midcourse Adjustments

Take time for some be-still-and-know-God moments. Don't ask anything. Just listen. Just be aware of His always-everywhere presence.

Where you are aware of a timing frustration, ask God to fill you with a *desire* to wait for renewed motivation.

Make this conscious adjustment each time you are tempted to ask "why."

The attitude I want to cultivate that reveals my acceptance is ——————————————————.

GROWTH DESIGN

Where I need to grow:

How I will know when I have grown:

What I plan to *do* today:

Chapter Four

More than One Selection

The year before purchasing my first car (the one with the well *and* spare tire), I walked. To work. To church. To the bank. To buy groceries. I gained exercise and lost weight. I learned to group trips and estimate how much I could carry in a four-block walk home. Limiting groceries to one bag was also economical. There was literally no room for impulse buying!

Actually, I thought I was very ecology-minded. Even when a sacker started to put a loaf of bread in a second sack, I requested: "Can't you fit everything into one sack?" He obliged, even though his I-was-only-trying-to-help-look disclosed his annoyance.

One Saturday I watched as my conveyor parade collected in the bin ready for the sacker. When the sacker had filled one bag, I suddenly realized that the end of my parade was still being checked at the cash register. I felt the embarrassed heat of one who had collected more groceries than she could financially cover . . . only worse. How do you reject groceries because you can only buy one bag's worth? As I pondered the walk home with two bags of groceries, I groped for a logical answer to the grocery boy's logical question, "Can I carry these to your car for you?"

"Certainly, just follow me up the street and let me buy one first!"

But retorts like that only come when I am trying to write a book! Instead, providentially my answer walked through the automatic door. "Debbie, did you walk? Do you need a ride home?" my friend asked.

"Yes! Yes!" I responded more automatically than the door that admitted him.

The incident taught me a lesson. The next time I bought groceries, I overcorrected and came home with only half a bag. But that created another problem. Have you ever struggled through a week with half a bag of groceries? Of course the alternative is simple: eat out!

Meeting shortages elsewhere in our lives is not as easy to resolve. Have you ever struggled through life with half of what you have the freedom to choose? Misjudging restrictions imposes unnecessary confinement.

It is especially true in my life as a single person. I have one grocery bag to fill: it's labeled "single." However, I don't always know how much I can put in it.

It was my senior year in college. There are a lot of ends in a senior year: an end to dormitory confinement, an end to back-to-back books with library intermissions. But ends give way to beginnings. Even though I knew I would be saying goodbye to friends and activities, and the security of a four-year routine, I was excited about my first career job, my first apartment, and most important of all, my first dream come true . . . marriage.

And then I came back to ends. To frayed edges and broken pieces. I don't remember when the differences between us began to erupt, but we started struggling to make our relationship work. We tried to be honest up to the point of ignoring the only option left: that our marriage was not to be. We faced that option one evening.

The room could have been romantic. Fiery fingers massaged burning logs. Dim lights sketched silhouettes in chalk. I stared evasively at the rug as if counting the two-toned loops. Bob sat on the couch, tense with impending decision. At the apex of this uncomfortable triangle was a professor and friend.

We talked. About what was right. About what was wrong. About bridging gaps. About broken bridges. And in the end, we faced just that . . . the end.

At first there was only the hole, the vacuum, the empty now. Tears didn't fill it, nor could friends or routine.

And then there was tomorrow. From the perspective of a painful today, tomorrow is either a promise of something better or the fear of continuing the same.

At this point, two very special people who helped me through some of those difficult days of beginning again, sent me a dolly gram. Have you ever received one? They are small stuffed dolls that pocket a message "Just for You." Ruth's special message for me was, "New worlds can be delightful."

Her words were prophetic, but, as prophecy goes, not immediately fulfilled.

It is difficult to see beginnings from painful ends. It is difficult to let go of what has been good before without a struggle to make it good again. But that struggle causes world wars: fearfully clutching to the past while desperately reaching for the future. I had to come to the place where I realized my world had not fallen apart; it had only changed. It was like a kaleidoscope. The colors were the same, they just fit together in a different way.

I realized I did not have to start my life over again. By kaleidoscopic turn, I was just continuing in a new way.

Then Ruth's words made sense. New worlds can delight with a freshness and uniqueness that exhilarates. Then I realized I could plunge myself into my new world without drowning.

But to accept God as a Bringer of Good out of all situations is not enough. I can't just sit around waiting for good things to fall from heaven. I have to accept some responsibility. I have choices to make. Of course, when everything entices, it is difficult to choose. That's why I take a small taste of everything at a buffet and end up with an embarrassingly full plate . . . and a stomachache.

On the other hand, I complain when it appears I have no choice. For example, dessert tonight will either be a chocolate chip cookie or a chocolate chip cookie. I can complain by wishing I had bought peanut butter cookies or oatmeal cookies and reject the whole plate. Or I can look for the biggest cookie with the most chocolate chips.

Remember: misjudging restrictions causes unnecessary confinement. It's the what-to-put-in-one-bag problem.

Too often I define single as the wrong kind of limit. Instead of regarding it as a temporary (perhaps permanent) description of my life-style, I think of it as a lid that limits, keeps me from happiness, love, fulfillment, success. Then I live up to the label "UNmarried" in all the *un* ways.

But there is more to being one than being un. For one reason or another I am single. It is a limit, not to keep me from, but to allow me freedom within. As long as I obey the boundary lines, I have more than one choice.

There are a lot of taken-for-granted areas of our lives where we make choices, not realizing the influence they wield in determining our life-styles. Singleness is a set of choices. The quality of life-style depends on the quality of choice. I don't have to feel like a pawn pushed around in a couples' world—not if I use my powers of selection to choose good things that will *add* to my world.

People add to my world. The people next door add occasional TV-sharing a la Marla's own peanut butter cookies. The people in my family add long distance love and support. The people in my classes add papers to grade and a reason to draw a salary check once a month. The people in my Sunday school class add an opportunity to share hopes and hurts within a Christian perspective. My world is not just a random sampling of people, even though there is variety. It is the result of choices.

I remember watching a TV program where a young boy came home from school devastated because "nobody will be my friend." He had the Robert Young Father-Knows-Best kind of dad. His father's words came from a loving heart: "To *have* friends you have to *be* a friend. Sitting on the sidelines waiting to be invited is not an act of friendship." The next day he brought home a smile and a boy named Ted. "Dad, meet my new friend. He likes to play first base and I like to play outfield, but we both like to win."

Have you ever sat on the sidelines waiting to be invited? I have. Especially on Sunday nights after church. Why doesn't someone invite me out? Don't they realize I don't have a car? Don't they know I have to go home alone, to an empty apartment?

But sitting on the sidelines waiting to be invited is not the way to add people to your world. I ignored my opportunity to choose another way to spend Sunday nights. I didn't want to give anything until after I had received. It seemed safer somehow. Safer, maybe, but more lonely. I can't tell you how limited my world was because of that attitude. And this time limited means with the lid *on*.

Last year I was involved in a drama workshop. One training exercise taught me more about what people can add to my life than about drama. A group of 10 to 12 people joined hands encircling one who was in the middle. The middle person was instructed to close his eyes and explore the territory by running, skipping, jumping, or falling. It was the responsibility of the circled group to protect the one in the middle from hurting himself. It was truly an experience in *community*. Of course, I am not advising us to live blindfolded. The lesson here is to select a support group that will involve me in community as an experience of sympathetic fellowship.

In the middle of writing this book, I moved. From one job to another. From one state to another. From one support group to one that I'm still in the process of building. I can't afford to wait for friendships to happen just because I'm new, just because I'm insecure, just because I'm single.

I also must keep in mind that I need all kinds of people in my world. Not just singles. For example, there has always been a person in my support group who, because of 40 to 50 years of proving God and His promises, can give me a better perspective against which to examine my pilgrimage. There has always been a family in my support group because I love family nights of TV and popcorn.

I feel especially privileged that my work with children has given me some special *young* supporters. I will never forget praying at the altar with Elizabeth. After we asked God to work out her concern His way, she asked me, "Can I pray for you now?" And teenagers . . . I still correspond with one girl whom I met as a teen-aged writer, speaker, leader. And she is still becoming more of all three.

Who do I blame because "nobody will be my friend"? Me and my sideline seat. It doesn't take money. It takes only a phone call.

Some choices have to do with money. Not just how to spend it. How to make it. And yet there is more to choosing a job than just getting a place in line at the cashier's window. I need a job that keeps me in a fulfilling world of people where the difference between the busy office and the silent apartment is not painful, but refreshing.

However, the classified ads with their professional needs have a way of overriding fulfillment needs. When that happens, we are caught in "until" jobs. I'll do this *until* . . . I marry, find something better, finish more education. Although "until" jobs can be important connectors in our lives, too often they establish unnecessary limits on how we spend our working time.

I found myself in an "until" job after college. I was in-between as a secretary. But I didn't spend four test-cramming college years plus one excruciating M.A. thesis-writing year to answer the telephone and brush up on my alphabet with filing. Don't get me wrong. No one has more respect for secretarial skills than I. Since I was not trained for them, the telephone and typing was my limit. Besides, I desperately wanted a job that would blend *my* strengths in a fulfilling way.

In the middle of this career query, I received a letter from my pastor. He wanted to specifically pray for his people. He wanted me to share with him by letter, my prayer needs. I did:

> Your letter reached me at a time when someone reaching out to care felt good. Thank you for your personal concern.
>
> I feel that I am in a time of preparation right now in my life. At times it seems as if I am standing in the middle of a merry-go-round world that is revolving without me. But I know that my perspective is never completely accurate. I face the same old problem that is forever new with each experience—What is God's will for my life today? I need desperately, work that will consume my interest and time. Creative challenge that will channel me in new avenues of service.
>
> So that's where I am . . . a time of restlessness . . .

59

a time of transition before the next major turn of my life. My human prayer is that a change will come soon. However, I know that God's good things are worth waiting for.

Sharing these thoughts with someone made me begin to see the difference between important transition and dangerous ruts. Transitional phases are important in our lives. Unfortunately, we sometimes label them as ruts.

A rut is not just doing the same old thing over and over. It is letting the same thing get old. If I don't look for new attitudes and new motivation as well as new processes and friendships, new is hard to find.

I have shared with many graduating seniors the benefits I did not see from in-betweening after college. I had an opportunity to get to know myself without the rigors of the collegiate schedule. For the first time in years, my evenings belonged to me for people, self-improvement, hobbies, *sleep!*

Recuperation is not the only purpose for in-betweening. The most important purpose is preparation. It is a time that is getting me ready to receive. If I am looking only for greener grass, I forget that the time to grow comes before the time to harvest. When I ask God to show me how to use in-between times, I will not just bide my time in a rut.

Sometimes we don't realize when ruts are the results of our own choices. If *where* I work is more important than the work itself, I may be limited by available choices. There is nothing wrong with ordering priorities that way as long as I realize the limits. For example, the job market is usually tight in a college community.

Another limit-line where career is concerned has to do with education and/or experience. I may need to commit myself to more education or accept a job just for experience to enlarge my possibilities. Remember that success is not only plotted on a vertical line, however. Not everyone can continue a vertical climb, because somewhere abilities peak. There is much to be said in favor of horizontal progress. It is not a rut if you are learning to do the same things in a new and better way. Remember?

And while I mention success and the push for it, don't forget that few people start at the top. We just hear about them after they get there. Listen to some success stories. If you want to be where John is, listen to how John got there.

Being single is not a rut where career is concerned. In fact it allows more extensive choices than we sometimes realize. I am one person choosing for one. I do not have to settle for less than fulfillment or less than adequate or above adequate salary just because I am single. However, I need to be willing to go where the jobs are. I need to remember that I have the time to accept a job that requires more than 40 hours a week. And if my job requires travel, I can enjoy being gone, free from guilt about home responsibilities. That is, unless I forgot to pay the electric bill before I left.

I remember when I was interviewed for my first college teaching position. I found this freedom to be an important asset. The dean was careful to explain that it was only a one-year appointment. There was a strong possibility that next year's arrangements might not include me. But I could afford to be temporary. I could afford to move in order to take advantage of one year's college teaching experience. I had only one person to transplant. However, as it worked out, that not-so-temporary job has been the catalyst for many other exciting career opportunities.

Job choices are part of what goes into our grocery sack. A positive work philosophy can help us color work days with joy and fulfillment.

Have you ever wondered what God's work philosophy is? I went back to Genesis 1 where we see God at work for the first time. I identified a work philosophy that promises His gift of joy and fulfillment.

1. *Know the work environment.* Most of us would have called "void" only empty space. But God saw the possibility of a world in the shadows. Perhaps I sometimes confuse the difference between work space and empty space.

2. *Produce the best with what you have.* Man, God's prized creation, was made from ordinary dust and an extraordinary Life-breath. With that record, what newness could God breathe into my work?

3. *Be innovative.* God wasn't satisfied with mass producing a few good ideas. Imagine how many different species He started with. God can teach me originality in my work when my imagination is committed to Him.

4. *Work to enjoy what you have done.* God's first words were creative. His second were statements of positive evaluation. "It is good," He said. To me He also seems to say, It is good to feel good about it.

5. *Save time for rest.* After a week of productivity, God reserved a day for renewal. I must remember that the weekend is for more than catching up on laundry, groceries, and car repairs. It is for renewal.

I believe God wants us to enjoy our work. Ecclesiastes substantiates this:

> *So I saw that there is nothing better for men than that they should be happy in their work, for that is what they are here for, and no one can bring them back to life to enjoy what will be in the future, so let them enjoy it now* (Eccles. 3:22).

To enjoy your work and to accept your lot in life—that is indeed a gift from God. The person who does that will not need to look back with sorrow on his past, for God gives him joy (Eccles. 5:20).

To enjoy your work, recognize it *is* a gift from God. Maybe that is why struggling to like my work is out of place. Of course I need to remember to make my life-arranging career choices within His choices for me. He does not ever condemn me to ruts. I need to be sure that my choices don't either.

There is one more very important selection I need to consider. *I can select an attitude.* I saved it for last because the wrong attitude can tear the bag and be responsible for losing all the other good grocery-bag choices. Attitudes don't just happen. They develop. If my attitude about being single is one that makes me think I am missing the "good life," maybe I am, because I have developed an attitude that says, I am a misfit, I am cheated. Therefore, anything that is here cannot make me happy.

It's time for Proverbs again: "A cheerful heart does good like medicine, but a broken spirit makes one sick" (Prov. 17:22). Now circle the "one" and read it again. It's true!

One day I was driving past a cemetery. It prompted these lines about an attitude responsible for a lot of brokenness:

> *Bent people*
> *Water roots*
> *With tears*
> *To cultivate*
> *Cemetery life*
> *From flowers,*

But in their hearts
They know
Tending flowers
Will not resurrect life.
How many times
Am I grave-tending
When, silent
In my mausoleum mind,
I reincarnate memories
As a synthetic substitute
For today.

Just as cemetery stubs
Mark yesterday life,
I must keep yesterdays
In their place,
Buried
Below the living level.
Useless grave-tending
Must give way
To life-mending
Because
Tomorrow begins today.

Living in the past is living backwards. With our thoughts and imaginations turned the wrong way, is it surprising that we fail to see any good in the future?

I know from personal experience it is not easy to let go of past things—like a love relationship. But I also know that I have to let go of it in order to build on it. Nor is it easy to keep from remembering past failure when I am struggling to succeed. But I must forgive myself for mistakes in order to learn from them.

Philippians 3:13 tells me to "forget past things." Forget whatever it is that slows my progress and discolors my attitude. Turn around. Look forward to what lies ahead.

Heinz catsup reminds me that good things sometimes come slow. Heinz will never win a catsup race because the characteristics that would make it fast would also destroy its goodness.

Even from catsup bottles we learn again that good things take time and quality is worth waiting for. In the meantime, "Be delighted with the Lord" (Ps. 37:4). Delight in His way that is beyond our dreams.

The past has its place in my life. But there is more to life than yesterday. As I delight in today and anticipate tomorrow, I can live with a forward-moving attitude. It is an important choice.

Where a yesterday attitude is backwards, a critical attitude is destructive. Criticism is a subtle boomerang. Negative words come back to the sender to grow a negative attitude. The result is more than dark night blight. It is an eclipse that keeps us from seeing the good in people, in situations, in ourselves.

God's Word is very clear about the standards we should follow in our communication:

> You have no right to criticize your brother or look down on him . . . each of us will give an account of himself to God. So don't criticize each other any more (Rom. 14:10, 12-13a).

> Some people like to make cutting remarks, but the words of the wise soothe and heal (Prov. 12:18).

And Eph. 4:25-32 deals with specific strategy: Focus on good words full of truth. Deal with grudges before the end of the day. Let love measure your words. Anything less is self-destructive because of our members-of-the-same-body relationship.

Therefore, just as God loves me even with His intimate knowledge of my strengths and weaknesses, I need to reflect His love with positive, encouraging words about people and ideas. Just as God encompasses my growth with His understanding of where I am and how much I can handle, I need to go the second mile in understanding another person.

I must choose to be positive. I must select good words. And the Holy Spirit promises to lead me in that Truth.

A positive attitude is more than covering up a negative one. It is important to examine causes, not the least of which are fear and worry. Sometimes it is easier to see what could go wrong and then be afraid it will and then worry about what you will do if it does. To prepare for the worst and then wait for it to happen is not abundant living! Not only does it require twice as much emotional energy, but it undermines God's sovereignty in our lives. How much do we really believe that God is in complete control? Fear and worry do not grow from confidence in God.

Psalm 56:3-4 reminds me: "But when I am afraid I will put my confidence in you. . . . And since I am trusting . . . what can mere man do to me?" These are David's words, probably composed while hiding in a cave from Saul's bounty hunters. What could mere man do? They were trying to kill him. Even though circumstantial evidence pointed to death, God had promised him royalty.

There have been times in my life when it looked as if people were getting in God's way. Instead of reaffirming my confidence in God, I thought about what mere man could do to my life and turned to fear and worry. One such time I wrote:

When I am sure of Your direction,
I expect others to be as sure.

66

Then to submit to human control
Seems God-defying.
And yet it is the way
You prove Your ominiscience
Once again.

There is another way to approach concerns and crises. Philippians 4:6-7 identifies the process: Pray. Tell God your needs. Not because He doesn't know them, but because you need to admit them. Then, look for answers. Thank Him that they are present even when you cannot see them. Accept His promise that when you do this, you will experience God-kept thoughts and a quiet, restful heart.

Not a bad way to live, as long as I have a choice?

There is one more takeover attitude that we can choose not to accept—bitterness. It roots deep before it breaks the surface. By then the damage has already been done. It grows from unresolved anger and I-have-been-wronged resentment. Unhealed pain can grow it. So can self-pity.

They were in love. Even though they had not yet said the words, they were aware of the feeling and the relationship. At least that's what Susan thought. Perhaps we will exchange the words tonight, she thought. But instead his words brought pain.

"I don't think we should see each other anymore."

Her first reaction was from hurt. "How could he do this to me? He had no right."

And then self-pity settled in. "Why? What is the matter with me?"

And then retaliation. "I'll show him. Nobody can treat me that way." The result: she found a quick replacement for her "love" and ended up saying the same painful words to someone else.

Hurting someone else does not heal personal pain. It just grows bitterness.

But it doesn't just happen with love or its loss.

Jerry was convinced he was next in line for promotion. Surely his on-the-job experience was as valuable as his performance record was commendable. Evidently the boss had other ideas. When the promotion announcement was released naming the company's veteran foreman as the new personnel manager, Jerry felt rebuffed. A short temper and cutting words were evidence of his private war. It was keeping good things from growing.

The Bible teaches us to: "Watch out that no bitterness takes root among you, for as it springs up it causes deep trouble, hurting many" (Heb. 12:15). Bitterness is another boomerang. And the one who hurts last, hurts most.

I have learned something very important about painful, crisis experiences. Sometimes the pain must happen to heal. After all, Ecclesiastes tells us there will be times in our lives when we will lose, and cry, and grieve. However, there is also a time to heal. Pain does not heal if bitterness is applied. Bitterness aggravates the wound.

The way to make sure that bitterness does not begin to root is to "fill yourself with God himself" (Eph. 3:19). As we are aware of the Holy Spirit's control in our lives we will bear His marks: "Love, joy, peace, patience, kindness, goodness, faithfulness, gentleness, and self-control."

I said earlier that being single is a set of choices. It really goes deeper than that. We live in a multiple-choice world where the freedom to choose is our privilege and multiple choice is the problem. We want life complete with happiness, fulfillment, and contentment. But sometimes there are blanks and missing pieces. We are frustrated not only by the confusion of choosing but of choosing right and living with our choices, right or not.

God does not leave me to play multiple-choice games. He offers ready counsel for every choice I must make whether it concerns friendships, jobs, or attitudes.

All I have to do is ask:

Dear God
Sometimes Your world is bright
With too many choices
And like a child in a toy store
I want to have it all.
Other times I am blind
To things within my capacity to choose.
Wouldn't it have been easier
If You had created me a robot
Mechanically programmed for perfect choices?
But You didn't.
In Your complete love
You have completely freed me
To choose.
Right now I admit my need for Your
      all-seeing
      all-knowing
      always right
        leadership.
So I wish to choose You back,
To let You choose for me.
And eliminate
Unnecessary choices.

Thank You!

GROWTH DESIGN

1. Circle It

Draw a circle to represent your single life, now. Think of three words that describe the way you feel about being single. Think of three words that would describe your feelings if you were not. Which words do you want to put inside the circle? Are there presently negative words inside? What choices can you make that would effect change?

2. Friendship Choices

How many in-the-same-town friends do you have in each age-group?

____ children   ____ middle-aged adults
____ teenagers   ____ senior adults
____ young adults

Choose one of the age areas where you have the fewest friends. How can you cultivate a friend in this area, this month?

Plan to call, visit, have lunch with, send a note to, sit in church with one friend in each age-group with whom you need to take an aggressive step in order to maintain the relationship.

3. Job Choices

Examine God's work philosophy from Genesis 1 in relationship to yours:

Know the work environment

What do I like about   What is within my ability
where I work: and authority to change:

Produce the best with what you have

I am doing my best in the following areas:

Where I need to improve:

Be innovative

Brainstorm some new direction, new method, new lines of communication that would add a freshness to your present job.

Work to enjoy

List the areas of your job responsibility:

List your strengths and likes in a job:

Draw a line where a job responsibility matches with a like or strength. What conclusion does this help you make about the enjoyment level of your present job?

Save time for rest

What are the "rest" activities you participated in last weekend? Make sure there is at least one evening that belongs to *you*. Consider it an appointment with yourself and protect it from outside intrusions as you would an appointment with anyone.

4. Attitude Choices

What is your attitude about the past?
   a. Glad it's over
   b. Wish I could relive it
   c. Hope nobody ever knows
   d. Trying to learn from it

If someone tape-recorded your conversations and re-played them, what attitude do you think would best summarize them?

    a. Positive and building
    b. Cutting and pessimistic
    c. Self-destructive

Are there choices you need to make that would bring about changes?

What part does memory and imagination play in growing bitterness? What prescription does Eph. 3:19 recommend?

GROWTH DESIGN

Where I need to grow:

How I will know when I have grown:

What I plan to *do* today:

Chapter Five

Love Is One Answer

It is Valentine's Day today. I even wore red to celebrate, but no one noticed.

Nor did anyone miss the valentine cards I didn't send this year. (I guess I say *this year* so you will think there was someone special to buy for last year. Don't be fooled. There wasn't.) However, I did notice all the people crowding around the card racks, trying to find a *personal* love expression from the hundreds of mass-produced "for my one and only."

I also noticed the Charlie Brown cards. Even browsed through them. Charlie Brown's long-distance love affair with the red-haired girl makes him a special compatriot of Valentine's Day. Certainly anyone with as much unrequited love as he had earns a Valentine's Bleeding Heart Award! On the other hand, as long as he sits during his lunch period with a paper sack over his head, unrequited his love will remain. Until love means "facing up" he will continue to sit on moonlight nights filling his "love is" list with wishful thinking:

Love is:

- Getting assigned the same lunch period as the red-haired girl.
- Getting used to wearing a paper sack.
- Finding out she likes peanut butter and banana sandwiches too.
- Having the courage to throw away the paper sack!

Sometimes I make a Charlie Brown "Love Is" list. Or rather . . . "Love, if I were married would be . . ." and then I fill the list with the ways I think marriage would make my life easier:

- Love is having someone to take out the garbage.
- Love is having someone tell you what is making that funny noise underneath your car's hood.
- Love is having someone with whom to take a crackly, October walk under an orange-slice moon.

What the list actually says, is that love is *having someone*. However, if my concept of love depends on wishful thinking, I don't know what true love is.

The first verse I memorized as a child contains my most important love lesson: *God is love*. When I was a child, I understood it as a child. Love was a name for God. I could call Him Love as easily as I could call Him God.

Somewhere in putting away childish things, I let go of the literal meaning of that phrase. I defined love outside of its Source. I based my understanding on a human relationship, an emotional feeling. But love is other than human. Love is God. It is His personality. First John 4:8, 16 reiterates it: "But if a person isn't loving and kind it shows he doesn't know God—for God is love. . . . God is love, and anyone who lives in love is living with God and God is living in him."

God is love. No one or thing escapes contact with His love. We can ignore it. We can refuse it. But like the spare tire, it is still there.

What if God stopped loving because of rejection? What if God withdrew His love from all people because some would not return His love? Then to think of love and God in the same word would be an inequality. Then love would be a game, and loving would be the heavenly pastime for some big cupid who had nothing better to do than engage in target practice.

But real Love in word and act is God in all His omniscience, in His always being everywhere. *God is love,* and He loves perfectly.

One of the transforming lessons of my young adult life came during a Bible study about God's love. The leader shared the thought that our response to life situations expresses the degree to which we really believe that God *is* Love and He *loves* perfectly. With His perfect love, He loves me more than I love myself. Because of His perfect love, He wants me to live a successful, fulfilling life even more than I want it.

Sometimes people wear paper sacks over their heads and think they know about love.

Janis sat across from me. A red-checked tablecloth was the appropriate decoration for our Italian meal of home-cooked lasagna. We were enjoying a catching-up time. It had been years since we shared each other's company. It is good to have a friendship that waits to be continued.

After we finished talking about family and friends and activities, she bared an emptiness within her. She was hungry for the assurance of God's love for her. The only way she knew to discover it was to try to earn it. However, busying herself doing "church" things to find God's love was the same as wearing a paper sack. She admitted to more confidence in her husband's love than God's love. It was a sequence or priority problem. There were steps to take and she had skipped an important one.

Remember working on research papers? Remember the difference between primary sources and secondary sources? If you want to know the way it really is, check out firsthand information. Go to the source.

The same is true with love. If I really want to know about love, I need to go to God. I need to experience His love firsthand. I need to learn from His perfect example. Otherwise I could learn the wrong things about love. I could learn that love hurts me. That love manipulates. That love is not to be trusted. And in my loving relationships with other people, I could communicate the same information.

The problem is a geometric one. The shortest distance between two points is a straight line. Human love can be part of God's love, but it is not the source. My face-to-face confrontation with *love* must go beyond my accepting His forgiveness for my sins. It must lead me into a love relationship with the Source of love that makes a difference in my day-to-day life.

How does God tell me that He loves me? How does my attitude about being single, about being the person I am, reflect that I believe God loves me? How does my spiritual growth demonstrate that I am aware that God is Love and that He loves me perfectly?

Sometimes it is difficult to read important messages. I am amazed at the facility with which a druggist reads my doctor's scribbled prescription. Where I see only hieroglyphics, the druggist understands meaning. The secret to communication is not in the handwriting, it is in understanding the field of reference.

How many love messages do we miss because we look in the wrong place for understanding?

My father is a tender man who is full of love for his family. That is not to say he puts his arms around me and with a penetrating gaze says, "I love you." He has his own way of communicating his love and it is different from what anybody else's father does. His love messages are private and in their privacy, they are special. For example, he knew I was going through some difficult days. His father-heart reached out to me by sending a book of poetry. In it he scrawled, almost illegibly, "I thought you might like this. Love, Dad." I could have reacted, "I don't need a book of poetry, I need his love." However, if I had focused on the *handwriting* I would have missed the message. Instead, I realized he was saying, "I know you are hurting. I want my love to help. I wish I could be there, but I can't; so I am sending this book to remind you that I love you." I am glad that love is tangible without black and white print. However, it is more than second-guessing and reading between the lines, because the interpretation is based on who I know my father to be.

The most important way that God communicates His love to me is by telling me who He is. The foundation for this communication is His recorded Word. As I understand more about who God is and that He wants to be all of who He is to me, I begin to realize that there is a height and breadth and depth to His love that has transforming power in my life.

As a Creator, God communicates His love. His character, His tastes, His philosophy are a part of everything He has made. There are messages in His world for me: object lessons telling me how He loves.

In retreats where I have been speaking, I like to involve groups in an activity I call "Wood Walk Wonder."

The name comes from a poem I wrote about a message
God gave me through His world:

> *A silent searcher*
> *In wood walk wonder*
> *I stumbled on Truth.*

More and more I am finding out that the world is a com-
muniqué from God. He has much to say to me if I take
time to read His messages.

It was a color-splashed September. One bush was
burning especially bright with September glow. As I
came closer, I realized that the leaves were in jesters' garb.
Half the leaf was green while the other half was marbled
crimson and gold. I realized that leaves in the process of
turning are beautiful. God's love holds me while I am
changing seasons. Farther down the way, a spider had
woven its silken net. It was early morning and dew drops
were like diamond ornaments. I saw how cobwebs, with
all those holes, hold water. I realized that God's love could
fill the gaps in my life with more than one thing.

I left the cobweb to begin a downhill trek. It was
rocky, steep, and difficult. Who said downhill is easy?
Downhill is harder, takes more energy, and makes me feel
more insecure than uphill. I felt God, in His love, counsel-
ing me to put away my fear of uphill plodding.

God speaks eloquently in every green and growing
thing. His love is a part of every color-coordinated season.
His world tells me that He gives beauty and balance to
everything He has made. His Word tells me that He loves
me more than birds or flowers.

Mercy is another characteristic of God's love that has
growing signficance for me. Over and over in the Psalms,
David talks about his merciful God. The historical record
of God's dealings with the children of Israel reminds me
strongly that God's love is full of mercy.

Mercy is a word-container full to the brim with meaning. Too often I have been guilty of looking at the container without exploring the meaning inside. The meaning of mercy expands my concept of God's love. Mercy is an act of love demonstrated when one has the power to hurt or destroy, but does not. It acts in behalf of a person to relieve and heal.

In a world where people who have the power to hurt or destroy, do; God who has all power, does not. His love is not a possessive destruction. His mercy will not allow it.

Isaiah was a spokesman for the judgment of God but not without tempering his words with the love and mercy of God. Over and over Isaiah told the people if they continued the way they were going with evil and ungodly ways, God's judgment would allow them to destroy themselves. If they repented and demonstrated their faithfulness to Him, God's love and mercy would protect and comfort them. Too many times his words fell on deaf ears. From a busy city corner he cried: "Come to me with your ears wide open. Listen, for the life of your soul is at stake. [God] is ready to make an everlasting covenant with you, to give you all the unfailing mercies and love that [he] had for King David" (Isa. 55:3).

Have you ever counted the mercies God showed David? David, protected from attacking lions and bears, victor in a mismatched duel with a giant, hidden from royal bounty hunters, reinstated king after an illicit affair. David understood God's mercy. His praise-songs connect God's mercy with love.

Psalm 103 reminds me not to forget the benefits of being loved by God. One of the best benefits is to experience the fullness of His mercy. I don't deserve His mercy in the measure He is willing to give it to me. But He doesn't remind me of my undeserving nature. He reminds me of

His willingness to love. He reminds me of the infinite "unlimit" of His power that He channels into His love.

Experiencing the mercy of God is to experience one of the richest characteristics of His love. It is not a permission to live any way I choose. Instead it is a way God makes it easy for me to choose His way of living so that He can show me all of His love.

To me, God's message of love is strongest as He tells me He is my Father. He is my Father through creation: "You made all the delicate, inner parts of my body. . . . Your workmanship is marvelous—and how well I know it" (Ps. 139:13-14).

He is a Father who takes responsibility in supplying protective security: "We live within the shadow of the Almighty, sheltered by the God who is above all gods. This I declare, that he alone is my refuge, my place of safety. . . . For he rescues me from every trap, and protects me" (Ps. 91:1-3).

He is my Father who listens and understands: "I keep right on praying to you, Lord, for now is the time you are bending down to hear. You are ready with a plentiful supply of love and kindness" (Ps. 69:13).

Of course, he could not be a true Father without being a disciplinarian: "After you have corrected me I will thank you by living as I should" (Ps. 119:7).

Although a human father may teach me my first concepts about fatherhood, my lessons about God's Fatherhood must not stop with humanity. Otherwise, I might transfer human characteristics to God.

John's father died at a time in his life when his self-identity was linked to a father-son relationship. Now all he had was a picture that would never grow gray hairs or develop wrinkles and the words from his mother and friends, "You're so much like your father." John didn't want to be *like* his father, he wanted to be *with* him. Without a head-of-the-household father, John took on more and more of the male responsibility roles.

He didn't realize how much his God-concept was reflected in his reaction to the absence of a human father. His father had left him to grow up on his own. As a result, there was an "on his own" attitude in his relationship with God. He seemed to be saying, since I can take care of home-things without my father, I can take care of life-things without God. It was not a rebellious attitude. It was incomplete understanding of the kind of father-love God has to give.

Human fathers, even almost perfect ones, can get cranky after a hard day at the office, can unconsciously ignore important questions while reading the evening newspaper, can misunderstand or not understand at all. And they can die leaving holes filled with hurt.

But God's Fatherhood is other than human. It is perfect. It fills gaps. It is always understanding, always aware of true needs and important desires, even unimportant wishes. And He will never leave me alone. When my relationship to God teaches me about His perfect Fatherhood, I am aware of how much He loves me.

What does this love say to me, a single person, who often feels the hole because of the absence of human love? It says that God's love fills my needs. It says that Love, real LOVE is a secure foundation that builds balance and harmony into my life.

And there are areas where balance and harmony are critical elements.

I remember a midnight talk with Terri during a retreat. Attractive, fun-loving, prank-playing Terri had a question that only love could answer. Feeling the need to be on her own, away from family and a frozen identity among people with whom she had grown up, she moved. A new city, a new job, a new set of friends helped her express the person she was growing to be. However, one well-meaning *married* friend passed on this haunting advice, "Now don't get *too* independent." Terri's question? "In a life-style that is saturated with freedom and independence, how do you keep from being *too* independent?"

Bob had all the trappings of a person with a put-together life who was on his way to success. His calm and comfortable authority gave him easy access to leadership. When he walked into a room, he was in charge by common consent. However, it was impossible for him to compartmentalize his gift of leadership to certain set-aside areas of his life. One day he admitted, "I have trouble letting God have complete control because I react as if it is a threat to my independence."

I have struggled with independence versus dependence more than once. I enjoy independence when it means not answering to anyone about what I eat or when I eat, where I go or what time I come home. I reject independence when it seems to isolate me by falsely implying, "I don't need anybody."

Sometimes it feels like a tightrope where leaning too far either direction causes a balance problem. If I fight a fear of independence by making sure people know I am dependent, I have not achieved balance. If I fight a fear of dependence by strongly expressing my independence, I am still off balance. Fear is a negative motive causing overreaction.

The goal for a life-sustaining love relationship is sometimes complicated by these independent and dependent needs. Some dependencies are life-draining parasites. Some independencies are self-destructive.

The one answer is *love.* Living within God's love defines the delicate balance. In Him I declare my dependence, because He is the source for all fulfillment. Through

Him I express independence in a way that will not hurt me or those around me.

Sometimes, for me, independence is too frightening, too stretching, too single. At those times, I remind myself that I am dependently independent. Paul realized the same truth when he said: "The less I have the more I depend on him" (2 Cor. 12:10).

Sometimes the word "dependent" evokes only negative, confining, restrictive thoughts. Then, I think of it as the difference between piggy-bank savings and investment with interest. My piggy bank is very independent. It protects everything I drop into the slot without any help from me. According to how many times I empty the loose change out of my billfold, the amount of money will increase. Because it is independent, the amount is never more than what I put in. However, if I take the money out of my piggy bank and place it in a savings and loan company, I can increase the original amount because I have made contact with a larger resource than my piggy bank.

Jesus taught this investment principle when he talked of a love relationship that meets *all* needs. He told His disciples: "Give Me your life and I will make more out of it than you could ever dream of. Invest it in Me, make contact with Me; depend on Me, then you will experience abundance, fulfillment, peace, joy."

God, whose first name is Love, relaxes the struggle between independence and dependence by being a need-filling Source. His love is constant and everlasting. I can depend on it. His love is perfect and productive. I can grow in it. At a time in my life when my needs vascillate between dependence and independence, it is important to know that I can depend on love to define the delicate balance.

Another area where it is easy for me to lose equilibrium is where fear is concerned. Fear and love cannot coexist.

Love in its wholeness, in its acceptance, in its security, and in its protection has no place for fear. And fear with its distrust, its negativism, its dread, its imbalance is against everything that love stands for.

The single life is often plagued with fears. There is the fear of being alone for the rest of your life, of having to raise children by yourself. There is the fear that love, found once, will never be repeated again. Fear: gnawing inside, preventing the enjoyment of aloneness because of loneliness, destroying my self-concept, clouding my future, infecting those around me with its negativism.

But fear and love cannot coexist. Moreover, Perfect Love has the ability to cast out fear: "We need have no fear of someone who loves us perfectly; his perfect love for us eliminates all dread of what he might do to us. If we are afraid, it is for fear of what he might do to us, and shows that we are not fully convinced that he really loves us" (1 John 4:18).

There was a time, not too long ago, when I was afraid that I was going to be single for the rest of my life. I was willing to admit I had enjoyed the freedom of single life for an extended period after college, but at 25, I had done more than I ever wanted to do before marriage. I was running out of ideas! The change of attitude came, not because I received a definite answer concerning whether I would marry or remain single. The change came when I no longer feared, when my relationship with Perfect Love cast out my fear. It was a matter of trust which involved an act of my will, called submission.

The will is one of the most unique human characteristics. It is where I have absolute control. God will not invade my privacy at the point of my will. I do what I choose to do. However, when I realize my inability to choose correctly, I should be smart enough to submit my will to One who can help me choose rightly. When I have complete confidence in His choices, I can enjoy complete satisfaction in His love. And that casts out fear.

Proverbs 29:25 wisely counsels, "Fear of man is a dangerous trap, but to trust in God means safety."

It is fear that Joe will beat me out of a job that I deserve which creates an eroding jealousy. And jealousy is a dangerous trap. It is the fear that if Steve breaks off our relationship, I will never find anyone else like him. If I react with insecurity and revenge, I am caught in two more dangerous traps.

Perfect love gets rid of fear traps because perfect love is freeing.

Since fear and love cannot coexist and since I can choose, isn't it reasonable to identify myself with love? Living within His love is to learn how His love casts out fear.

There is one more way in which love meets me where I am in order to take me where I need to be. It fills the empty gaps and holes in my life.

I used to think that holes were meant to be filled. Somebody told me to fill nail holes in my apartment walls with toothpaste. Then I had to be careful not to hang anything in the same place, not to mention getting used to a Colgate air-freshener fragrance. And who cares how jeans' holes are patched? Neither the material, the texture nor even the color have to match. Only the size. However, some holes can't be filled with just anything.

I worked on a jig-saw puzzle the other night. I always think it will be easier to find a piece after a complete outline has been defined. Wrong! I spent 15 minutes looking for one piece. I tried pieces that "almost fit." Some were proportionately larger or smaller. Some were jigsawed exactly opposite to the way I needed them to be. Until I found the right piece to fill the hole, there was emptiness. Anything but the right piece spoiled the picture and the misplaced piece created another hole somewhere else in the puzzle.

Holes in my life are the same way. Not everything can fill them. Some holes can never be filled. They just have to be there with their emptiness. I accentuate the emptiness if I focus on the hole. I can waste a lot of time looking for something that will fill it. Or I can direct my focus on another part of life's puzzle, realizing that in the process of putting the pieces together, I will eventually find the right piece for that once-baffling situation. Perfect love fills holes because perfect love helps me find the right pieces.

Of course, the love of which I speak identifies a spiritual relationship with God. It does not disregard a need for human love, but it does supercede it because God's love can *be* more and *give* more than human love. Is there a single adult who does not dream of a perfect love, an always-present relationship, an always-adequate, always-need-filling involvement?

Where I want love, I can have *real* love. And real love fills the holes in my life better than anyone or anything. Besides it prepares me in the best possible way for loving relationships with other people.

There are many areas of need in my single life, but I am learning that there is one answer. It is an answer that tells me who God is and who He wants to be to me. It is an answer that defines the delicate balance between independence and dependence. It is an answer that casts out fear and plugs up holes. That one answer is LOVE and it is the answer for every one.

The answer comes when I "experience this love for [myself], though it is so great that [I] will never see the end or fully know or understand it. And so at last [I] will be filled up with God himself" (Eph. 3:19).

The answer comes from the primary Source, God himself. If I miss love from the primary Source, is it not likely that I will miss love from secondary sources? First-person contact with love forever changes my love for someone else, whether it is the neighbor-love for all I meet or the special love reserved for husband and wife. It is *real* love that makes the difference in my life. It is *real* love inside me that makes it possible to live by the 1 Corinthians 13 standard: courtesy, kindness, patience, always positive, never selfish or jealous.

At a time in my life when it is easy for me to think I am living without love, God says, "I am Love. No one else will ever be able to mean love the way I mean it. That is why anyone living in Me is living in love and it causes them to live in love with people and all creation." It is a romance with life that makes many other romances worthwhile and productive.

> *Dear God*
> *Balance me in Your Love*
> *That I might not*
> *Fall from high-wire teeter.*
> *Cast out fear*
> *That makes me less of who I am*
> *By misunderstanding who You are.*
> *Fill my holes*
> *That gape like earthquake fissures*
> *Waiting for someone or something*
> *To make the pieces fit.*
> *And remind me always*
> *That You authored love,*
> *And for any experience to mean love for me*
> *It must involve a first-person relationship*
> *With You.*
> *It is always the answer that I need.*
>
> *Amen.*

Growth Design

1. Love Is . . .

What characteristics are usually attributed to love? Can you add to the list?

a good feeling   understanding
a magnetic attraction   acceptance
happiness   a fluttery heart
security   an emotional imbalance
blind   an idealistic panacea

Now substitute *God* for *love*. Cross out the characteristics that do not belong to God's love. Are you living with any untrue definitions?

2. Geometric Love

The shortest distance between two points is:

In learning about God's love, that means:

3. Wood-Walk-Wonder

Read Psalm 104. Fill in the following:

God's creative power at   How I need this creative
work in His world.   love-power in my life

Take a wood-walk-wonder (even if it is just looking out a window). Look for a symbol of His message to you. If possible, bring back a tangible object as a reminder. Finish the following:

This _____ tells me God is love

because _____.

Matthew 6:30 reminds me that _____
_____.

4. The Lord Has Mercy!

Think of an example where someone with authority used this authority to your disadvantage. How is God different?

Where do you need to feel God's mercy to heal where someone or something has destroyed or hurt?

5. God, the Father

Think of an example where your father or another person's father disappointed or hurt you. What do Ps. 68:5 and 103:13 say about God's fatherhood?

Where do you need His Father-love?
    to help you understand how you are made? (Ps. 139:13-16)
    to remind you how secure His protection is? (Ps. 121:1-4)
    to listen as well as understand? (Ps. 69:13)
    to help establish the discipline you need? (Ps. 54:4)

6. A Declaration of . . .

Fill in the following:

	Advantages	Disadvantages
Independence		
Dependence		

The best of both is experienced by total yielding to God. According to Matt. 10:39; 16:24; and Luke 9:23:

What do I lose?

What do I gain?

7. Phobias

List three fears you are aware of in your life. Finish the chart as the example indicates:

Fear	Focus	Method for Overcoming	Changed Focus

GROWTH DESIGN

Where I need to grow:

How I will know when I have grown:

What I plan to *do* today:

Chapter Six

One Whole Person

Monday night a whole chocolate pie graced the make-shift bookcase-buffet. It was tempting in its uncut completeness. However, before the evening was over, my guests devoured all but one piece.

"Do you want half of this?" my roommate asked the next night.

"No, you can have the whole thing," I replied, as if wholeness was an honor I could bestow.

However, if I believe that wholeness means taking advantage of all that is really there, perhaps it is. The fact that seven-eighths of the pie was gone, didn't make the last slice any less whole.

People who feel fractioned because of wishful thinking are living less than abundantly. And single people who are more aware of holes than wholeness are not learning that *one is more than un through oneness.*

Jesus came to make people whole. He brought physical, emotional, and spiritual wholeness. The woman who touched the hem of His robe was made whole. The man whose hand was withered like an October leaf was made

91

whole. Legion, emotionally handicapped, demon-possessed, was made whole.

However, the story that has real significance for me is the story of the crippled man beside the Bethesda pool.

Jesus asked him, "Would you like to be whole?"

The man replied, "But I can't. The angel must move across the water before I can be whole."

Jesus didn't ask him why he couldn't be whole. He simply asked, "Do you *want* to be whole?"

"But I can't," the man reiterated. "No one will carry me to the pool. And even if I could get there, someone is always there before I am. And only the first one in is healed."

He missed the point again. Finally, Jesus simply gave him instructions: "Roll up the pallet on which you have been lying, get up, and walk."

The Bible says he was instantly made whole.

This incident teaches me more than the fact that Jesus has the power to heal. It uncovers three keys to wholeness.

1. *The first key to wholeness is immediate obedience.* My brother climbs mountains. Not molehills. Real, cloud-pricking mountains. More than once he has been on rocky ledges where the difference between up and down was a life and death matter. One time he was edging precariously along a rocky ledge when a friend called in a not-to-be-ignored voice . . . "STOP!" He didn't ask any questions or expect to understand the full background of that command. He stopped . . . just in time to see the rock that was supposed to support his next step, crumble like a cookie. The timing of his obedience was important to his remaining whole.

Obedience is inseparably linked to the wholeness of the abundant life. "Obey all the commandments of the

Lord your God, following his directions in every detail, going the whole way he has laid out for you. Only then will you live long and prosperous lives" (Deut. 5:32).

What happens if I do not obey? I put myself in a position to receive less than God designed. Less than all is not the way to wholeness.

This obedience has special implications for a single adult. Trying to find the missing seven-eighths of my pie is not the way to achieve wholeness. Obedience is. Immediate obedience.

There are acts of obedience and there are attitudes of obedience. Where they come together, they harmonize in praise: "Thank you for this day, this life, my personhood, my singleness." I know people who have been afraid to thank God for singleness for fear God would interpret it as a desire to remain single. It is a fear that shows an incomplete understanding of a God who creates abundant life. It is the result of reacting toward singleness as a *part,* a very *small* part.

Singleness itself is neither part nor whole. It is my attitude toward it that can be less than whole. I don't believe there is any merit in resigning myself to singleness. There is only merit in a willingness to accept the steps by which God is leading. There is merit in a willingness to accept future steps without trying to decide what those steps might be. It is a matter of obeying today and planning to obey tomorrow. Dwelling on the what-ifs of tomorrow because I am afraid I may not be able to obey Him, separates me from God's best for my life.

Jesus came to make people whole. He came to demonstrate that a daily obedience, in thought and act, releases the energy and motivation to obey tomorrow. He was obedient unto death. But on the third day came resurrection, a new kind of wholeness.

2. *Put away the sign of your handicap.* What if the man who had running legs restored to him had said: "I probably shouldn't get up right away. After all, my muscles are shriveled up from disuse. Why, I could sprain my ankle leaping for joy! I better hang onto this bedroll a little longer." Jesus predicted this human reaction. He told the man to put away the thing that symbolized his handicap.

Sometimes we too easily let our "bedrolls" of the past remain. Jesus asks us, "Do you want to enjoy oneness? Do you want to be made whole?" Rather than answering yes, we present our excuses:

But I can't . . . I'm single. I won't be fulfilled as a person until I marry.

"Do you want to be made whole?" Jesus asks.

But I can't . . . my job is not satisfying to me.

"Do you want to be made whole?"

I can't . . . things just aren't going the way I thought they would.

Just as with the man at Bethesda, God is not interested in listening to our excuses. He gives us the same instructions: "Roll up the sign of your handicap, take My hand, and let's walk . . . together."

I met Sarah at a retreat. Sarah was diabetic. I never saw her take an insulin injection. I didn't have to. She told me all the things she couldn't do and couldn't eat because she was "handicapped." For her, wholeness seemed an impossible distance away so she accentuated the signs of her handicap. She tried to find security in people knowing about her condition. But it was false security. Wholeness for her would come when she could allow the simple identification tag around her neck to be the only necessary sign of her handicap.

Tom was divorced. Sometimes I think too openly. He created his own name tags with phrases like: "Before I was divorced . . . My ex-wife . . . People think divorced

94

men . . ." The ease with which he lived with his divorced identity was not a sign of wholeness. He was comfortable calling himself divorced because it was a scapegoat for his feelings of incompleteness. He could blame nonacceptance in the church on his being divorced. He could blame dead-end dating relationships on the fact that girls didn't want to go out with a divorced man. It was a sign of his handicap, a "bedroll" that separated him from expressing wholeness.

How do you put away signs of handicaps? Sometimes very slowly. Sometimes all at once. God writes the orders for recovery. He knows me well enough to pace my putting-away time. I can trust Him. When I am not depending on signs of handicaps for security, I can depend on God. The result is wholeness.

Probably the most important key to wholeness is the last one:

3. *Allow God to create wholeness His way.* Perhaps this is the most important key of all. I don't believe that the Bethesda man really wanted to be crippled. That's why he sat, day after day, by the pool of water. He knew his chances were 1 out of 1,000, but it was the last possible chance he could think of. He never imagined that the prophesied Messiah would come during his lifetime and walk past him as he sat hoping to find healing from the Bethesda pool. It never occurred to him that the very Son of God would instantly heal him. But that's the way it happened.

No matter from how many sides I look at a people problem, a family problem, a Christian growth problem, I won't see it from the all-knowing perspective of an all-seeing God. I need to remember to count Him alive and at work in my behalf to help me experience wholeness.

Before I realized how Jesus wanted to bring wholeness to my life, I rested on bedrolls that prevented it. I struggled with unnecessary crutches that prevented my finding the oneness God wanted me to have as a single adult. I still struggle with some. My faith muscles atrophied when I mistook the picture I saw to be the whole truth. But only God sees the whole picture. Only God gives wholeness to life.

Knowing what the steps to wholeness are and then taking them is sometimes the difference between oneness and un-ness. I can point to several things in my life that have caused the difference.

One of the things that can keep me from being wholly one is what I call "puzzling." It happens when I react to the possibilities of my life as puzzle pieces. With my overactive imagination, I take the possibilities of my life and try to make a picture. Since I want God's design for my life, I take the puzzle picture and lift it up for God to approve.

"See, God? Is this the way you want the picture of my life to be?"

The silence confuses me. I assume it means my picture is wrong. I take the picture down to look at the pieces again. Why, of course! Why didn't I think of that before! This piece doesn't go here, it must go there.

After rearranging a few more pieces, I take my changed picture and lift it up to God.

"Now, is that better? Is that the way my life is going to be?"

Still no answer. I take the picture down again. This process continues as long as I can endure it. All this time, God patiently waits, interested in my "puzzling." Then when I run out of ideas, I react like a child who is exasperated because his desire to make the puzzle fit exceeds his skill to do so.

"Here, I can't do this. You do it."

That is just what He was waiting for. When all of the

pieces are in His hands, He gives them back to me one by one and shows me how they fit together. Then, I begin to see a picture I never thought possible. One that far exceeds the 101 possibilities I mathematically figured.

Puzzling. We have all done it. We've puzzled over jobs, romances, opportunities. It is a step past the logical process of analyzing options because if the situation doesn't develop as I figured it would or ought to, I come face-to-face with disappointment. And that's the culprit that prevents my oneness.

Disappointment reflects the inadequacy of the human perspective.

"We can make our plans, but the final outcome is in God's hands" (Prov. 15:1). Another paraphrase might be: "We can dream our dreams, but the best dream God envisions."

Just like the Bethesda cripple, our inability to see all the possibilities keeps us paralyzed. When we become emotionally tied to a dream that doesn't come true, when we try to jump ahead of God by puzzling, the result can be disappointment and frustration in varying degrees of intensity. It is my fault though I seldom accept blame for it.

It's because I'm single . . . If I were married . . .
It's because of my boss . . . If he would . . .
It's because of my roommate . . . If I could just . . .

It never occurs to me that my humanly narrowed picture causes the lump of disappointment that unsettles my stomach, sags my face, and tears my eyes.

We need someone who can see past today and beyond ourselves. God meets those prerequisites. He does not choose that we experience disappointment. He wants us to enjoy oneness. Therefore He desires to plan for us. His ideas for our lives are always more fantastic, more creative,

97

more fulfilling, than our wildest dreams. And we are all dreamers!

Disappointment is a relatively mild emotional imbalance. If we allow it to fester, however, it develops into depression—a culprit responsible for preventing oneness.

One night I was sound asleep when the telephone rang. My reflexes, operating without a wide-awake brain, pulled me out of bed and made me stumble through the darkness to the telephone. It was a long distance, *collect* call. A male operator made me very suspicious at 3:00 in the morning. I made him repeat the information. While I was trying to decide if the call was legitimate or a prank, I heard the broken but familiar voice of someone I knew.

"Debbie, it's me," she said.

I knew something was wrong and accepted the charges.

"Darlene, what is it?"

In the staccato rhythm of someone who had more to say than her tears would allow, she told me how lonely she was. She couldn't stand it any longer. She had to talk with someone.

Depression seriously separates the single individual and prevents him or her from enjoying the oneness that God intends.

I could astound you with statistics of depression-related suicides. I could share reports from psychiatrists and mental hospitals that scare us with the emotional imbalance in our society. But I'm not trying to say, "Join the club." On the contrary, I'd prefer you cancel your membership by way of *active* understanding. That means by *doing* something about what you understand!

Depression, by definition, is a hollow place, a decrease in force and activity, a state of being pressed down. But I know how to define depression without looking in a dictionary. My journal entries from the year following my broken engagement are shrouded in a black notebook, and not by accident:

4-13-71

> *There has been an earthquake in my life.*
> *I want to cry*
> *But no tears come.*
> *I want to be violent*
> *I want to beat against a wall to say*
> > *I have had enough*
> > *I am tired*
> > *Let me alone*
> > > *Or help me?!*
> *It takes time and tears and darkness*
> *To pull broken pieces together.*
> *I know there is no anesthetic for this pain—*
> *It must happen to be over.*
> *So if it must be,*
> *Then let it be.*
> *But soon . . .*
> *Let it be over.*

I can pat myself on the back when I have a good reason for depression. People are full of sympathy when crisis comes. However, there aren't many pats for a typical dark-night depression. A more recent entry:

> *I am writing, this having just left my dampened*
> > *pillow to throw away tears in Kleenex.*
> *Tonight, it is difficult to be single.*
> *Tonight, waiting is hard.*
> *I went to the party . . . alone.*
> *Surrounded by couples*
> *I was singularly quiet.*
> *I came home . . . alone.*
> *Silenced by the stillness*
> *Alone I feel I'm half of what I should be.*

Tonight my perspective is too narrow.
My generalizations, distorted.
I don't want to harm anyone with them,
Especially not myself.

What can I do about depression? Let it happen? Call it one of the occupational hazards of being human? Of being single? Let it run its course?

No. The risk is too great. I am too important to God to let depression chisel me down to less than I can be. Therefore, on days when the sun is shining, inside and out, when motivation peaks; when I know *and* feel *there is more to being one than being un* . . . that's when I decide what to do about depression.

I have found four guidelines that help me take an objective look at depression. I wouldn't call them "Four Easy Steps to Depression-free Life," however! Each step requires that I stop and look past what I am feeling to see the situation for what it really is. I must realize that it can help me instead of hurt me and strive to understand how. Each requires that I be willing to eliminate negative thinking patterns. Each will help me realize that *there is more to being one than being un.* I don't have to be satisfied with halves because God wants me to enjoy wholeness. He promises to provide a way . . . sometimes of escape, more often of endurance.

1. *Identify depression patterns to uncover the real causes.* When am I most often the victim of depression? At night? When I haven't had enough sleep? On rainy days? During the winter? When I am undergoing unusual amounts of pressure? When I experience hurt, rejection, or failure, no matter how minor? Because I am afraid?

We tend to blame other individuals. Too often we fail to take responsibility for our actions, shifting the blame to someone or something else. It is easy to blame depression on loneliness, on being single, on having to go home to an empty house, on trying to be two parents in one. It is more difficult to stop the thoughts that apply pressure to the dangerous areas of insecurity, fear of failure, or feelings of unworthiness or unimportance.

I find that conversations with myself help—aloud (but in the privacy of my own apartment, of course). I divide the dialogue between my objective self (the part of me that tries to see the situation from the outside) and my subjective self (the part of me that tells it like it *feels*). For example:

Objective Self: This is not one of your good days is it?

Subjective Self: No. I'm lonely. I'm on the verge of tears. I can't bear the thought of being by myself tonight. Why doesn't someone notice? What's wrong with me?

Objective Self: How is your deadline coming for the play to be produced in one week?

Subjective Self: Everything that could go wrong is going wrong. Nobody is meeting deadlines. I had two people with major responsibilities drop out today.

Objective Self: Then loneliness is not your problem, is it? You feel wronged by people in whom you trusted responsibility. Since your position will not allow you to take it out on students, you are punishing yourself.

Subjective Self: I guess so.

Objective Self: Then what can you do about it, tonight?

Subjective Self: Nothing. That's what really bothers me.

Objective Self: Right; and it will continue to bother you as long as you keep thinking about what you can't do.

101

I guess I adopted this method of working out negative feelings because there isn't always someone to talk to. Rather than bottle them up, I bounce ideas off myself. It is a way I learn to accept my feelings while being careful to identify real causes. It is a way in which I learn that rationalization is only a local anesthetic. Like having a shot of novocaine, when it wears off the real pain starts. Therefore I have tried to train myself to be objective about the causes and patterns of depression. I must believe that I am stronger than one dark night's feeling of weakness. I am more successful than the debit ledger for one day. I am more appreciated than my own emotional tally.

2. *Determine a plan of action to alleviate depression.* I can usually trace about 50 percent of my depression times back to fatigue. I don't see things clearly when I am tired. I am most likely to make wrong assumptions about how bad the situation is, how big the problem is, how impossible the job is, when I'm tired. Of course there is an easy solution to a fatigue problem: get some sleep! It is amazing the solutions I find after a night's rest or the strength and motivation that is renewed.

However, when I am suffering from fatigue-related depression, going to bed early makes me feel like I am admitting defeat. Therefore, I postpone sleep as if playing a game to prove my competence. But psychological games don't produce winners. Instead of gaining competence, I deepen depression.

There is one exception to this strategy. Some people dangerously use sleep as an escape. For them, a more positive plan of attack is necessary to restore balance.

A fresh look at myself and my situation can stop the depression cycle. A 30-minute drive sometimes does as much good as a weekend trip. Also, I find soothing inspiration from watching how nature copes with environmental forces.

Recently I watched a tree being teased and tossed by a blustery wind. Its leaves fluttered like the pages of a book. But instead of remaining stiff and unbending, it's supple branches relaxed to allow the huffy violence to blow through—bending perhaps, but not breaking. I watched a stream unconsciously adapt its course to the changing design of the river bed without frustration. It flowed over and under and around the obstacles of rock, fallen limbs, and debris without an arrogant push or self-inflicted paralysis. Its strength was consistency; its beauty, poise.

Have you ever accidentally interrupted the business enterprise of an expanding ant hill? Watch how those busy insects meet crisis. There is momentary bewilderment but immediate and intense reconstruction activity. They seem to be created with an inherent initiative to begin again.

Depression will increase if I don't do something about it or find someone else to help bring me out. The emotional energy I consciously apply to alleviate depression is less than what I lose if I allow depression to run its course. What am I saying? Don't just sit there feeling sorry for yourself . . . *do something!*

Not long ago, I was puzzling over a matter and wound up with self-inflicted disappointment which was expressing itself as depression. I knew what I had done. I asked God to forgive my fumbling, but that didn't get rid of the feeling. I had a choice. I could mope around, stare at the TV, feel sorry for myself, try to placate my feelings by treating myself to a hot fudge sundae (which I didn't need), or I could *do* something.

I didn't feel like cleaning out the closet, but I knew that it would release emotional tension. Going through stacks—organizing, filing is therapeutic for me. Perhaps it is analogous to the reorganizing that is going on in my thinking process. I also know that if I *do* something, if I have something tangible to show for my efforts, I foster

103

positive feelings. Besides, when I look back on the day, I do not remember the emotion, I remember what I did about it.

During emotional roller coaster rides, I have worked on writing files, teaching files, bulletin boards, craft projects. I have scrubbed walls that didn't need scrubbing, rearranged furniture, tried a challenging recipe. It takes my conscious will. I repeat: I don't *feel* like doing anything. I have to *make* myself do it. However, because it diverts my distorted look at what is happening, because it postpones my analysis of the situation until I am able more logically to handle it, I am able to find a oneness that God wants me to have.

3. *Recognize the difference between the factors within your control and the factors outside of your control.* I have no control over another person's decision, the unbalanced ratio between men and women, or death. Those facts in a given situation are constant. It is my reaction to those facts that can place me on an emotional seesaw. If I look for something to change in my situation, I could be in for a long wait, depressing my emotions one notch lower.

Take my first apartment. (And I wish you would have!) The living room rug was soap-suds-gray and the bedroom rug was stepped-on-pink. Even when I added my blue and green personality accents, it was a flimsy camouflage for incongruency.

"How do you like your apartment?" my friends innocently asked.

I'm not sure they were ready for my list of grievances. I blamed my apartment for many attacks of loneliness and depression.

Of course, no one shoved the apartment down my throat. I signed the lease of my own free will. And because I had signed, my apartment was going to be a constant for

104

at least nine months. Any amount of emotional energy I spent on wishing it away was wasted. The challenge was to do something about the factors I *could* change.

I asked the Holy Spirit first of all to help me change my damaging attitude. Then I put myself into some decorating projects. I wouldn't call the result a face-lift, but it definitely helped. Besides, it was rewarding and, therefore, therapeutic to see a situation I had improved by my own efforts.

"All things work together for good." That scripture is not just a pat answer. It is true. There is good in every situation. Oneness comes from allowing those good factors to come together and create wholeness in ourselves. The alternative is that they could work together for bad and cause disunity. But God desires that they work together for good.

One other point is important here. I have learned something about emotional crises or debilitating attacks of depression. Sometimes pain must happen if there is to be healing. However, pain does not heal when bitterness is applied. Bitterness aggravates the wound. "Watch out that no bitterness takes root among you, for as it springs up it causes deep trouble, hurting many" (Heb. 12:15).

4. *Realize that the factors outside of your control cannot hurt you when God is in control.* If anyone knew about being depressed because of uncontrollable factors within a situation, David did. He testified: "On the day when I was weakest, they attacked. But the Lord held me steady. He led me to a place of safety, for he delights in me" (Ps. 18:18-19). On another occasion he reported: "The very day I call for help, the tide of battle turns. My enemies flee. This one thing I know: God is for me" (Ps. 56:9).

If I believe God is who He says He is, then He is all

these: Light, Peace, Love, Hope, a Perfect Father, a Perfect Counsellor, a Merciful Judge, an Always Present Friend, a Healing Physician, an Understanding Brother.

If I believe that God is who He says He is, then He isn't darkness, frustration, struggle, depression, hunger, thirst, heaviness, impatience.

If I believe that God is who He says He is, that He is all-powerful and that He will use His omnipotence to act in every situation for my good, *then why don't I act like it?* Why do I act as if God is someone He isn't? Whatever way we react to God doesn't change who God is, because we can't change Truth. However, our reaction can change us. Our reaction can separate us from God's design. It can keep us from being all that we can be—from being *one,* from being *whole.*

I never thought that a group of squirming, frustratingly lovable children in junior church would give me an important discovery to share with singles, but they did. I asked a circle of third-graders to tell me why they loved God. I'll never forget what Christina said: "I love God because He's *really* God."

That's where I need to respond to God's call to wholeness . . . by believing that He is really God and acting toward myself, toward my life, toward my future in ways that prove I believe He's really God.

Do you believe He is really God? Does your belief in Him affect every level of your life? Does that belief make you comfortable in His timing, His plan? your singleness? How closely is your mental and emotional acceptance of His really being God aligned with your actions?

He came to be really God to me so that I could experience the wholeness, the oneness with Him that Christ had. Consider this prayer of Christ as a prayer for the single adult: "My prayer for all of them is that they will be of one heart and mind, just as you and I are, Father . . . I have given them the glory you gave me . . . the glorious unity of being one, as we are—I in them and you in me, all being perfected into one" (John 17:21-23).

I am not half because I am single. God calls me to be one . . . to be wholly and completely and perfectly one. I may act as half and if I marry, then I take half a person into marriage. But marriage needs whole people, too.

When I believe that God is really God, when I allow Him to be really God to me, when I take all of myself and give it to Him so that He can fill me with All of himself, then I can truly say:

Nothing can separate me from the love of God	or cause disunity
Death can't	even the painful death of dreams or forever-gone yesterdays
Life can't	the single life I experience now, the tomorrow life I am waiting for.
Our fears for tomorrow	whether I will marry or remain single; whether I will obtain or maintain financial security.
Our fear for today	Can I pay the bills? Find someone to eat dinner with? Make my job deadline (or whatever my today-fear might be)?

Nothing will ever be able to separate me from the love of God . . .

Except myself and my wrong, negative thinking.

"Make it your aim to be at one in the Spirit and you will be bound together in peace" (Eph. 4:3).

O God
You have called us to be whole.
You have called us to enjoy Your good gifts.
Open our eyes wide enough to see
the beauty, joy, and goodness
You have given.
Let that beauty, joy, and goodness
help us achieve the oneness You desire for us.
Whatever is separating us,
keeping You from being really God to us,
Whether it is a
weak self-concept,
festered worries about a job or money,
fears about tomorrow;
Whatever it might be about being single
that would appear to keep us from
allowing good things to work together,
Open our eyes in a new, wide way
So that we may be able to feel and understand
how long
how wide
how deep
how high
Your love really is and
To experience this love for ourselves
So that at last we will be filled
Wholly
With all of You that there is.   *Amen!*

GROWTH DESIGN

1. Handicap or Wholeness?

Read John 5:5-9.

What excuses did the crippled man give Jesus?

108

How did his excuses handicap him?

2. Define

If a handicap is a real or imagined obstacle, define wholeness:

Where do you feel more incomplete than whole?

Are there reasons or excuses for this incompleteness?

3. Regimen for Recovery

Immediate obedience

Take an obedience test based on one of the following verses: Matt. 5:22, 25, 44; 6:3; 6:25; 7:1.
Ask the Holy Spirit to bring to your mind a situation where your obedience needs to be more immediate. How can you decrease your reaction time and increase your reaction response?

Beyond bedrolls

Where are you experiencing a handicap?

What are the signs or demonstrations of this handicap?

Use Matt. 6:34; 1 Cor. 12:9-10; Col. 2:9, to write a prescription for yourself that will enable you to live "beyond bedrolls."

Allow God to create wholeness

Where have you most recently been "puzzled"?
From Ps. 32:8, what does God promise in this situation?

From Ps. 37:34, what does God ask from you?

4. Active Understanding

Depression patterns

I usually blame _____ for my "down" times.

These "down" times usually occur _____.

It is possible that _____ is the real cause of such times.

Prescription

Write out your own prescription for the next depression attack:

A matter of control

Consider one of the areas where you are experiencing incompleteness. What are the factors within your control?

What are the factors outside of your control?

How can you focus on the factors within your control?

Recommit the out-of-control factors to God.

5. Who Is God, Really?

Based on the following references, who does the Bible say that the Triune God is? List these characteristics under "Who God Is." On the other side of the chart, identify the opposite characteristic.

Reference	Who God Is	Who God Isn't
John 8:12		
Isa. 9:6		
Ps. 103:13		
Ps. 50:6		
Matt. 28:20		
Matt. 8:16		
Jer. 30:17		
Ps. 147:5		

Is there an area where you have been reacting as if God is someone He isn't?

Is there an area where you need to experience more of who God is?

GROWTH DESIGN

Where I need to grow:

How I will know when I have grown:

What I plan to *do* today:

111